Praise for
God the Father Revealed

"This book has made me feel so loved by God. I would definitely recommend this book to people questioning God's goodness!"
—Catherine Christie, Hope Ranch for Women Residential Coach

"Humbly, Lewis presents an open dialogue that explores God's heart, intent and purposes. I believe Lewis' lifelong devotion to scripture memorization, Biblical life application, and Godly character have given him a voice we can listen to, and together explore beyond the surface of scripture the nature of our Heavenly Father."
—Steve Miller, China Harvest

"Lewis Erickson leads the reader on an amazing journey through scripture that stimulates the heart and mind to a new level of understanding of God's heart. *God the Father Revealed* will have a profound positive impact on anyone seeking God for the first time, or a person seeking a deeper relationship with God."
—Jim Neice, Pastor, Great Plains Church of Wichita

"God is longing for men and women who will know and understand Him. Let God use these pages to help you to do that!"
—Kary Oberbrunner, author of *Day Job to Dream Job* and *Your Secret Name*

"I love how Lewis Erickson looks at the whole of scripture with one idea in mind - God is good. And in so doing he uncovers one gold nugget after another revealing just how good God really is. For instance, when the Bible says we hear God in a "still small voice," Lewis explains that it's because God wants us to get really close to Him - so close that we can hear Him whisper. Whoa! The nuggets in the story of Abraham's call to sacrifice his son, were enough to buy the book. It made me want to keep reading. Seeing God as good as Lewis presents indeed "changes everything." Thank you, Lewis for sharing your insights with us all!"

— Mark Oelze, creator of PLEDGEtalk,
and author of *The PLEDGE of a Lifetime*

"From the beginning of time God has longed to be Father to His Children. Lewis Erickson invites you to discover just how much God the Father loves you and desires intimate relationship with you. Through God the Father Revealed, your heart will come alive as you receive the bounty of God's grace and truth that will set you free."

—Cathy Turner, Hope Ranch for Women Founder & CEO /
Christ Church Associate Pastor

GOD THE FATHER REVEALED

Understanding and Knowing Him Changes Everything

LEWIS ERICKSON

God the Father Revealed © *2019* by Lewis Erickson.
All rights reserved.

Printed in the United States of America

Published by Author Academy Elite
P.O. Box 43, Powell, OH 43035
www.AuthorAcademyElite.com

All rights reserved. This book contains material protected under International and Federal Copyright Laws and Treaties. Any unauthorized reprint or use of this material is prohibited. No part of this book may be reproduced or transmitted in any form or by any means, electronic or mechanical, including photocopying, recording, or by any information storage and retrieval system, without express written permission from the author.

Identifiers:
Library of Congress Control Number: 2019912991
ISBN: 978-1-64085-896-1 (paperback)
ISBN: 978-1-64085-897-8 (hardback)
ISBN: 978-1-64085-898-5 (ebook)
Available in paperback, hardback, e-book, and audiobook

Unless otherwise indicated, Scripture quotations are from The ESV® Bible (The Holy Bible, English Standard Version®), copyright © 2001 by Crossway, a publishing ministry of Good News Publishers. Used by permission.
All rights reserved.

Scripture quotations labeled NKJV are taken from the New King James Version®.
Copyright © 1982 by
Thomas Nelson. Used by permission. All rights reserved.

Scripture quotations labeled KJV are from the
King James Version of the Bible.

Scripture quotations labeled NIV are taken from the Holy Bible, NEW INTERNATIONAL VERSION®, NIV® Copyright © 1973, 1978, 1984, 2011 by Biblica, Inc.® Used by permission. All rights reserved worldwide.

Scripture quotations labeled NLT are taken from the Holy Bible, New Living Translation, copyright ©1996, 2004, 2015 by Tyndale House Foundation. Used by permission of Tyndale House Publishers, Inc., Carol Stream, Illinois 60188. All rights reserved.

Scripture quotations labeled TLB are taken from The Living Bible copyright © 1971. Used by permission of Tyndale House Publishers, Inc., Carol Stream, Illinois 60188. All rights reserved.

Any Internet addresses (websites, blogs, etc.) and telephone numbers printed in this book are offered as a resource. They are not intended in any way to be or imply an endorsement by Author Academy Elite or the author, nor does Author Academy Elite or the author vouch for the content of these sites and numbers for the life of this book.

CONTENTS

Preface 1
Introduction 3

PART ONE – A WALK THROUGH GENESIS

1 Genesis 1–4: The First Turning of the Other Cheek 11
2 Genesis 6–10: Hitting the Reset Button 21
3 Genesis 11: Fill the Earth 25
4 Genesis 12–14: Blessed, But Do You Know It? 31
5 Genesis 15: Fear Not! 35
6 Genesis 16: God Always Sees Me 45
7 Genesis 17: One Step at a Time 51
8 Genesis 18: Your Father Is *the* Judge 61
9 Genesis 19: Judge, Jury and Executioner 73
10 Genesis 20: He Takes It Personally 83
11 Genesis 21: It Comes to Pass 89
12 Genesis 22: How God Felt 95

13	Genesis 25: Turning Things Upside Down	105
14	Genesis 26–36: Holding on	113
15	Genesis 37–50: Working All Things Together	125
16	Judah: From Wickedness to the Heart of Jesus	131

PART TWO – PERSONAL STORIES

17	A Lopsided Game	137
18	Much More Than Puppy Love	141
19	A Cricket in Your Hair?	149
20	God's Refrigerator Art	155
21	Come to Me!!	159

PART THREE – PUTTING IT ALL TOGETHER

| 22 | One God | 169 |
| 23 | Conclusion | 179 |

Appendix A – How to Become a Follower of Jesus... 183

Appendix B – Discussion Questions 185

Acknowledgements 187

Notes 189

PREFACE

The inspiration for this book came from a message I gave as a guest speaker on Father's Day 2017, "What is Our Heavenly Father Really Like?" I had people tell me that it favorably changed how they thought of God the Father. Then it hit me: if people don't understand God, it must be difficult for them to truly love and trust Him. It would tremendously change people's lives if they truly understood and knew God. But how do I tell people? That's how this book began.

I thought I would cover the entire Old Testament in this book just as I briefly did in that 2017 message. However, as I studied more, I came across more and more material just within Genesis that should be included. This wasn't new information. Rather, it was information I had glossed over while reading it for roughly 50 years that now seemed new and amazing to me. I'd now found enough material concerning God's character and personality in Genesis alone for an entire book! That's how I decided to focus on Genesis and include other verses when it will help our understanding. Like a tour guide, I want to point out things about God that you and I may have missed before, but once you see them, they will change how you view God forever!

While writing this book, I was reminded of past personal experiences that opened my eyes to God's unique perspective on me and the world. I decided to share these complementary stories in this book to reinforce what Genesis was saying about God. A few of these personal stories were unique enough and could be read with several of the Genesis stories, so I decided to present them as separate chapters and group them as Part Two.

I've tried to write this book so that it will speak to anyone. Whether you're a mature Christian or know little about God, if you desire to know God, this book should be of great help.

I strongly encourage you to read the Bible along with me. I list the Bible chapter(s) to be covered in the chapter titles. It may appear that I am skipping parts of the Bible. I only do this because the scope of this book is learning about God, not all the people in biblical history. Like the proverbial beggar telling another beggar where to find bread,[1] I am only human. Please don't accept the things I say without checking them yourself first.

Take time to ponder what you've learned after reading each chapter. God is a complex being. You are a complex person. For you to experience the complete level of personal transformation I believe you can have from knowing and understanding God, skimming this book won't suffice. Invest in yourself. Take the time to think through what is being presented. Most of all, talk to God after each chapter and ask Him to open and increase your understanding of Him. Tell Him you want to know Him. See what He does!

Reading this book may be like building a house. When building a house, you don't start with the good-looking parts like colorful paint. You first must lay some foundation materials like concrete and dirt. Those aren't pretty, but they're necessary for the house to stand. The house won't be pretty for a while until the finish materials like windows get installed. Finally, comes the colorful paint at the end. In the same way, this book must lay some foundation materials about God before we can build on that foundation. It may seem slow or obvious to you at times. Don't give up. The colorful part will come!

Enjoy the book. Enjoy your God!

INTRODUCTION

Jesus told many stories to get His point across to His listeners. One such story went something like this:

A man went on a long trip. Let's call him Joe. Before leaving, Joe gave his wealth to three servants to manage for him while he was gone. When he returned, he asked them to report to him what they did with it. Two of them invested it and doubled Joe's money. He praised them for their actions and gave them more to manage.

The third servant did something unusual. He buried Joe's money in the ground! The servant told Joe that Joe was a hard man, taking the earnings from investments for himself. He was afraid of Joe and buried Joe's money instead of doing anything with it. Now that Joe was back, the third servant gave him his money back.

Joe was livid when he heard this. Joe could have buried it himself if he didn't want to do anything good with the money. Joe told the third servant that he should have at least deposited it at a bank so Joe could receive his money with some interest. Since the servant did nothing with it, Joe fired that servant on the spot.[1]

What a story! The third servant obviously didn't *know* Joe very well, nor *understood* what was important to him. He probably thought he *knew* Joe well. He even told Joe that he *knew* Joe to be a hard man. He judged Joe to be unfair when Joe received the earnings on his money that someone else had invested. He thought he should get to keep the profits and Joe should be happy just to get his money back. This servant found out the hard way he didn't really *know* and *understand* Joe.

Joe was angry with the third servant for judging his actions. In Joe's eyes, it was his money that was to be invested. Joe thought he should be the judge of how he rewarded those who invested it, not the third servant.

Do you see how the third servant's perception of Joe caused him to act irrationally and resulted in a bad outcome for himself? Just as the servant messed up his life because he didn't *know* and *understand* Joe, many people in real life mess up their lives because they don't *know* and *understand* the person who gave them a life in this world to invest: God. And since they don't *know* and *understand* God, they judge Him to be hard and unfair, not realizing how good and loving He is. "People ruin their lives by their own foolishness, and then are angry at the Lord" (Proverbs 19:3, NLT).

> **And since they don't *know* and *understand* God, they judge Him to be hard and unfair, not realizing how good and loving He is.**

A major purpose of this book is to keep you from repeating the mistake of the third servant. It is to help you know and understand God; to appreciate Him, love Him and enjoy Him.

Can we really find God? Is "knowing God" even possible? Does He want us to know Him? This is what God says about that in the Bible:

- "I would not have told the people of Israel to seek me if I could not be found." (Isaiah 45:19, NLT)
- "And no longer shall each one teach his neighbor and each his brother, saying, 'Know the Lord,' *for they shall all know me*, from the least of them to the greatest, declares the Lord.

For I will forgive their iniquity, and I will remember their sin no more." (Jeremiah 31:34, italics added for emphasis)
- "I want you to know me more than I want burnt offerings." (Hosea 6:6, NLT)

Yes, if we choose to believe what God has said, we can find and know God.

Jesus took this a step further when He said He would reveal the Father: "No one truly knows the Son except the Father, and no one truly knows the Father except the Son *and those to whom the Son chooses to reveal him.*"[2] Jesus reveals what God the Father is really like so that we can know His Father. Jesus demonstrated that it was His desire we know God the Father when He prayed, "And this is eternal life, that they *know* you, the only true God, and Jesus Christ whom you have sent."[3]

God says that understanding and knowing Him is to be valued more than other things in your life: "Thus says the Lord: 'Let not the wise man boast in his wisdom, let not the mighty man boast in his might, let not the rich man boast in his riches, but let him who boasts boast in this, that he *understands* and *knows* me, that I am the Lord who practices steadfast love, justice, and righteousness in the earth. For in these things I delight, declares the Lord.'"[4]

I don't know about you, but the three things God has told us not to boast about (wisdom, strength, riches) are the three things many of us *do* boast about. In fact, we all spend a tremendous amount of our time, money and energy in pursuit of wisdom, strength and wealth. But God says that there is something much more important to value than these: to *understand* and *know* Him. Wow! Can you imagine understanding God? Understanding why He does what He does? Can you also imagine knowing God?

There is an old saying, "Be careful what you wish for; you may just get it." In the same way, you may avoid looking for God because you are afraid of what you could find:

- God from the Old Testament may scare you. He has killed people with fire and plagues before. You may remember hearing of Him being angry with people.
- You may believe God will want you to do things you don't want to do; like wear long hot robes, sing chants or live in a grass hut far away.

If any of these fears are what you are feeling, I urge you to keep reading. I believe those fears will have been overcome by the time you have finished this book.

The God of the Old Testament and the God of the New Testament are the same God. God didn't have a personality transplant in the 400 years between when the last book of the Old Testament was written and when Jesus came. Jesus meant it when He said, "Anyone who has seen me has seen the Father."[5] It was God the Father who sent Jesus to Earth.[6] We wouldn't know anything about Jesus, and Jesus wouldn't have come here on Earth if the Father had not sent Him. So, if you like what you see in Jesus, you will like what you see in God the Father.

You may not have had the best of parents, or perhaps even no parents at all. Chances are that any bad impressions that you have of your parents, especially your Earthly father, have been subconsciously projected in your mind to God, your Heavenly Father. Do you find yourself saying or thinking, "I'm just not good enough"? Maybe your father pushed you about not measuring up to his desires or never gave you any indication of his approval. Maybe he was never around when you needed him. Maybe he didn't treat you like you would have wanted, even abused you. Perhaps that's why you recoil at the thought of knowing God, your Heavenly Father.

A Bible verse that has encouraged me to seek God is Proverbs 25:2, "It is the glory of God to conceal things, but the glory of kings is to search things out." While God has concealed many things about Himself, He never intended that they be hidden forever. Did you get that? Like a father who plays "hide and seek" with his children, He wants us to find Him. God says in Jeremiah 29:13, "You will seek me and find me, when you seek me with all your heart."

Through this book, we are going to look for Him. My prayer is that as a result of what you read in this book, that you will find God. In finding Him, you will begin to understand and know Him. Not like you would know historical facts about a U.S. President that lived 200 years ago, but like you would know a best friend. Once you truly know God in an experiential way, you will delight in Him more than anything else.

God is by far not the only person who plays a role in the Bible. In fact, a lot of the Bible, the Old Testament in particular, reports on the actions of various people who were evil and did things God did not approve of. Yet they are mentioned in the Bible to provide examples of what not to do.[7] Unfortunately, when some people read the Bible, I sense that in their disgust for the actions of these other people, they somehow include God the Father in their disgust, almost like guilt by association. Just like we would not like to be associated with all the bad acts of humankind since creation, let's not associate God the Father with all the bad acts in the Bible.

God can be found. He can be known. He wants you to find and know Him. He created you for that purpose. Will you begin your search for Him?

As my family says when we play the game hide-and-seek, "Ready or not, here we come!" God, we know you are ready and waiting for us. Here we come!

PART ONE
A WALK THROUGH GENESIS

CHAPTER 1
GENESIS 1–4: THE FIRST TURNING OF THE OTHER CHEEK

Can you imagine creation being any better or more beautiful than it is today? When you see a whale breach the water's surface and make a tremendous splash as it re-enters the water, the splendor of that can take your breath away. When you walk on a nature trail or on a lush green tropical island, the beauty of what you see is just amazing. Can you imagine what the world and everything in it was like when God had just finished creating it?

The very first verse of the Bible states, "In the beginning, God created the heavens and the earth."[1] The rest of Genesis 1 goes into some detail of all that God created. As you read through the chapter, you will come across one phrase that is mentioned numerous times, "And God saw that it was good."[2] He evaluated everything that He created and said it was good. The plants, the animals, and all of it, what He created was good. That is an important thing to remember: What God creates is good. That includes you and me too.

Unfortunately, it doesn't mean that everything stayed good, does it? But when He originally created it, it was good.

In Genesis 3, the one and only thing God tells Adam and Eve not to do, they end up doing. I often get mad at Adam and Eve when I see suffering and pain taking place in this world, because if they hadn't disobeyed God, all of us wouldn't be suffering today like we do. But, in their defense, if I were in their shoes and they were in mine, they would be getting mad at me because I would have probably made the same mistake.

Now Adam and Eve had someone encouraging them to disobey God. He was called "the serpent"[3] in Genesis 3, but we know him today by the name of Satan. "But the serpent said to the woman, 'You will not surely die. For God knows that when you eat of it your eyes will be opened, and you will be like God, knowing good and evil.'"[4] The first part of what Satan said, "you will not surely die," was the opposite of what God had said to Adam earlier. Satan cleverly redirects Eve to "doubt first God's word and then God's goodness."[5] He leads Eve to believe that God was keeping something good from her and Adam. At that moment, Adam and Eve were presented with the dilemma of who to believe. Unfortunately, they chose to believe Satan and not God.

This is an important point. Some of us have read through this story in Genesis so many times in our lives and don't think much about it. The story line of the entire Bible is based off this dilemma of who to believe. Will we believe God or someone else?

The story line of the entire Bible is based off this dilemma of who to believe. Will we believe God or someone else?

Will we trust God or someone else? Will we doubt God's goodness? Unfortunately for humankind, Adam and Eve chose not to believe God back then. Humankind as a whole, more often than not, chooses not to believe God today.

Their unbelief caused them to sin against God. What does it mean to "sin"? Sin is defined in I John 3:4 (KJV) as "transgression of the law", so sinning in this context would be transgressing [breaking, not obeying or rebelling against] the law [commands] of God. When we don't believe God, it is inevitable that we also will find ourselves disobeying Him.

Now bear with me for a little bit longer, as humankind is not the focus of this book. However, I do need to make one more point about them. When Adam and Eve heard God walking in the garden, rather than run *to* Him, they ran *from* Him. Why? Adam explained by saying, "I heard the sound of you in the garden, and I was afraid, because I was naked, and I hid myself."[6] They were ashamed. They were embarrassed. They were exposed. All because they were naked. They didn't realize they were naked earlier during all the other times that they had been with God. They were just as exposed then as they were any other time, but now, suddenly, they realized they were exposed, and they felt ashamed and embarrassed.

Now that we have finished setting the stage, we can finally get to the point of this chapter: God is good, kind and compassionate. This book is about learning what God is really like, so let's see now how God responded to all this mess that humankind made of the perfect world that God had created.

We read in Genesis 3:21 that "the Lord God made for Adam and for his wife garments of skin and clothed them." Why did God clothe Adam and Eve? Was it because God didn't want to see their nakedness? No. God already knew what they looked like. He made them! He made them naked, and He had been meeting with them that way ever since they were made. I believe the reason He clothed them was so they wouldn't run from Him. With clothing they wouldn't feel exposed in His presence. They wouldn't be embarrassed and run away from Him.

Why would it matter to God whether they ran from Him or not? I believe it mattered to Him because He wanted to be with them. He wanted to talk with them. He created them to have relationship with Him. The same goes for us. He created us to have relationship and communicate with Him. It matters greatly to God whether or not we have a relationship with Him.

What else do we see in this verse that God did for them? He provided for them. He didn't say, "Hey, Adam and Eve, you go find and kill something and make a garment to cover yourself so you can come to Me and then we can hang out." No, instead God went to the effort of creating the "garments of skin" and "clothed them." God provided those garments for them. Prior to this, Adam and Eve had somehow sewn fig leaves together to cover themselves,[7] but I doubt that they lasted very long at all. God had not designed leaves to work as clothing.

Can you imagine the maker and ruler of the universe going out of His way to provide these garments to Adam and Eve? It wasn't His fault, nor His problem, yet He was the one cleaning up the mess that Adam and Eve had created. Why would He do that? Why would He not start over with new people, Adam and Eve version 2.0 back in the garden of Eden? That's what we would have done. It was because He had chosen to love them as they were and wanted nothing to get in the way of them being able to come to Him. To continue relationship with them, He had to turn the proverbial "other cheek" that Jesus talked about.[8]

All of these developments greatly changed the order of how things had been. Up until then, humans and animals had only eaten plants.[9] I am assuming that if all animals ate plants, then there was no need for either humans or animals to kill another living thing. So, where did God get the "garments of skin" that He used to clothe Adam and Eve?

He could have spoken them into existence like He did the rest of creation, but He had finished creating creation. So, I believe He took the life of living animals to get the garments of skin. My belief is founded on the Bible's use of the term "garments of skin" implying the skin of some other living animal. So, an important Biblical principle

> **This principle is that not believing God leads you to disobey God**

GENESIS 1–4: THE FIRST TURNING OF THE OTHER CHEEK 15

is brought to light in this area of the Bible. This principle is that not believing God leads you to disobey God, and the final result of that is death, either your own or someone else's death.

Let's keep moving to Genesis 3 to read about one of the saddest days ever in biblical history.

> Then the Lord God said, "Behold, the man has become like one of us in knowing good and evil. Now, lest he reach out his hand and take also of the tree of life and eat, and live forever—" therefore the Lord God sent him out from the garden of Eden to work the ground from which he was taken. He drove out the man, and at the east of the Garden of Eden he placed the cherubim and a flaming sword that turned every way to guard the way to the tree of life.[10]

You're probably wondering why God drove them out of the garden if He wanted relationship with them. He had clothed them, so they weren't ashamed to come to Him anymore. Why now kick them out of the garden? How is that going to help His relationship with them?

It's good to ask questions when you read the Bible and don't understand something. That's the best way to learn! God won't be offended that you ask. Instead, He will be delighted that you are wanting to search for Him enough to ask tough questions. Remember our quick reflection on Proverbs 25:2 in the Introduction of this book, "It is the glory of God to conceal things, but the glory of kings is to search things out." Let's search this out.

I believe the reason He banished them from the garden is if they ate from the Tree of Life, they would live forever. That's actually what God says He is concerned about in Genesis 3:22. So that begs an even more interesting question: If God loved them and wanted a relationship with them, why would He not want them to live forever?

Let's clarify something first. He did want them to live forever. But to answer the question, if they lived forever after sinning against

God, then anyone else who had sinned against God should also get to live forever. Who else had sinned against God?

The Bible tells us that before Adam and Eve sinned, Satan also sinned and then led one-third of God's angels in a revolt against God.[11] That revolt failed, and these former eternal angels of God were sentenced to eternal death in the lake of fire when Judgment Day arrives.[12] Until then, some were kept in chains until Judgment Day[13] and others were cast from heaven to earth. They loiter around looking for ways to afflict humankind, the object of God's affection.

If Adam and Eve ended up living forever by eating from the Tree of Life, then God, if He wanted to be a fair and just judge, would have to choose between allowing Satan and his angels to live forever too, or punishing Adam and Eve with the same punishment that had been decreed for Satan and his angels. With Adam and Eve not living forever, God's promise of death if they ate from the tree of the knowledge of good and evil is not broken, and Satan can't accuse God of being an unjust judge. Meanwhile, God can carry out His plan to redeem humankind so we can still live forever with God. We will learn more about this plan later in this book.

God, in doing something that seems mean in banishing Adam and Eve from the garden was actually acting in love in order to keep His relationship with humankind intact. Just like any good parents or any people who really love you, they may have to do something that feels harsh and mean in order to do what is best for you in the long run.

Moving on to Genesis 4, there is a series of discussions between God, Abel and Cain. Some of them are recorded here, and others are not recorded but are implied. For example, how did Cain and Abel know what was an acceptable offering to God if God had not had an earlier conversation with them sharing what was an acceptable offering? So, if that conversation took place but wasn't recorded in the Bible, that probably implies that there were other conversations between God and humankind that were not recorded in the Bible either. With all that in mind, it appears to me that God was still in relationship with Adam and Eve even after expelling them from the garden of Eden. That relationship just was not taking place in the garden anymore. He went with them out of the garden.

To confirm the thought that God went with them out of the garden, let's focus on the first part of Chapter Four. Cain has just murdered Abel. God has just confronted Cain about it. God says that the ground has swallowed up Abel's blood and, as a result, the ground won't yield food for Cain any longer. Cain laments the judgment God has placed on him by saying, "My punishment is greater than I can bear. Behold, you have driven me today away from the ground, and from your face I shall be hidden."[14] For Cain to say that he shall be hidden from God's face as he wanders the earth (that was Cain's conclusion of his punishment, not God's necessarily) implies that he had access to God's face before his judgment was carried out. In addition, that statement means that he valued the Lord's presence and lamented that he would be leaving that presence as the consequence for killing Abel.

The first four chapters of Genesis reveal important aspects of both God's and humankind's character:

- God created something very good.
- Humankind messed it up by choosing to believe someone other than God.
- God went out of His way to cover humankind's nakedness so they would not flee from God's presence due to their embarrassment and guilt.
- God banished them from the garden so they can't eat from the tree of life. While harsh, He did that so He can be a fair judge, keep His word from being broken, and keep alive the plan that humankind can still live with Him forever.
- God went with them when they were expelled from the garden.

- Humankind continued to sin more regardless of what God did to help.

Wow! How does God seem to you now? To me, God seems to have gone to a lot of trouble to maintain a loving relationship with humankind in these first four chapters of Genesis, more than He had to and more than we deserve. But that's what people do when they love someone as much as God loves us.

What causes you to run from God? What keeps you from running to Him and makes you run away from Him instead? Is it your failures? Is it a feeling that you've let God down in the past? Do you feel exposed or embarrassed whenever you think about God or try to get close to Him? Maybe just like Adam and Eve, someone has told you some lies about God. I want you to think about these questions for a minute. Just dwell on them. Ponder all that God did for Adam and Eve. Doesn't it sound like God went to great lengths *after* they had sinned to maintain a loving relationship with them?

God went to all this trouble because He wants to be with us. Later in the Bible, He explains the reason for this. It's because He loves us and wants us to be with Him forever.

Please don't lose sight of this amazing fact. God didn't run away from them! God didn't abandon them! Neither did He give up on them! That's what people do to others who let them down, but that's not what God did. Instead, He went to them to help them. That's not how we normally think God acts with people who sin like we do. But that is what God did *and continues to do today*.

If you go to Him, He won't turn you away.[15] He wants to help you and draw closer to you. Let's pause for a minute to thank God for loving us even with all our sins and problems.

This book began with a desire to seek God in order to find Him so that we can know Him. After seeing how God acted in these first four chapters of Genesis, how He continued meeting and talking with Adam, Eve, Cain and Abel outside of the garden of Eden, this encourages me that God wants to be with us. He wants us to find Him. He desires a close relationship with us.

We have learned some important things about our God already, and we've just barely scratched the surface. There's a lot more to see in our quest to find, understand and know Him!

CHAPTER 2
GENESIS 6–10:
HITTING THE RESET BUTTON

I don't think I'm going to surprise you when I tell you that God hates wickedness. But do you know *why* God hates wickedness? Is God like every other human king, president or dictator who just wants his or her own way? Or is there another reason? One you haven't considered? I want you to understand why God hates wickedness because it will reveal something good about Him, which will help you know Him better.

In Genesis 6, Adam and Eve have had many sons and daughters, and several generations have come and gone. The number of men and women on the earth has quickly grown. We find God at this point upset and in tremendous despair.

> The Lord saw that the wickedness of man was great in the earth, and that every intention of the thoughts of his heart was only evil continually. And the Lord regretted that he had made man on the earth, and it grieved him to his heart. So the Lord said, "I will blot

out man whom I have created from the face of the land, man and animals and creeping things and birds of the heavens, for I am sorry that I have made them." But Noah found favor in the eyes of the Lord. (Genesis 6:5–8)

This is the first time that the word "wickedness" or the root word "wicked" is used in the Bible. Using the Strong's Concordance Hebrew Dictionary,[1] the Hebrew root word for "wicked" means "to spoil (literally by breaking to pieces)." Now we know part of why God was so distraught. Humankind was "spoiling" and "breaking to pieces" what He had worked so hard to create. It might help us understand the depth of God's feelings if we personalize this by putting ourselves in His shoes, so to speak.

Have you ever had something you created of great value destroyed by someone else? I saw a poor family on the news who lost their home to an arsonist. The tears they shed from their loss and the anger they felt for the person who destroyed what they had worked so hard and for so long to build seemed overwhelming, to say the least. With them in mind, now I think we have a better picture of what God may have been feeling at that time.

The Bible says in Genesis 6 that God's heart was broken. He had a broken heart! Have you ever pictured God being hurt before? Ponder that for a moment. The Almighty God, Creator of everything, hurt with a broken heart! Unfortunately, this won't be the last time that God is hurt by humankind. In Ezekiel 6:9 (NLT), God says about the Israelites, "They will recognize how hurt I am by their unfaithful hearts and lustful eyes that long for their idols." While we can never hurt God physically, when we reject Him and choose to love other people or things in place of Him, it does hurt God, because He loves us. His heart was broken by humankind back then. I believe His heart still breaks today.

> **His heart was broken by humankind back then. I believe His heart still breaks today.**

In Genesis 6:11–13, we learn more of how God may have been feeling: "Now the earth was corrupt in God's sight, and the earth was filled with violence. And God saw the earth, and behold, it was corrupt, for all flesh had corrupted their way on the earth. And God said to Noah, 'I have determined to make an end of all flesh, for the earth is filled with violence through them. Behold, I will destroy them with the earth.'"

Because of humankind's wickedness, not only had they corrupted what God had created, but they were filling the earth with violence. I take that to mean that humans were killing and hurting other men and women, and not just occasionally. The Bible says that "the earth was filled with violence." There's no way to know if this is more or less violence than we have in our world today. But what's important here is that God felt the earth was filled with violence and felt there was no chance of recovery. He had no choice but to hit the reset button and start over with the one man who pleased Him: Noah.

Genesis 7 and 8 deal with the flood, but I want to stay focused on what God says about violence. In Genesis 9, God spoke to Noah and his family after the floodwaters had receded and they had left the ark. Of all the things God could have told Noah and his family coming off the ark, He basically tells them three things.[2] Our focus will be on the third item:

1. Be fruitful and multiply. Fill the earth.
2. The entire animal kingdom will fear you and they are given to you for food, except you may not eat their blood, for the life is in the blood. (Animals had spent a lot of days on the ark with Noah and his family. They probably became comfortable around humans. Therefore, God gave them a fear of humans when leaving the ark to help protect them.)
3. Whoever kills a human being, whether it be a man or beast that does it, God will require a reckoning. Humans shall end the life of anyone who kills another person, for when they kill another human, they kill someone made in God's image.

Unlike with the animal world, God breathed His own breath directly into Adam. Of all living things, humankind was unique in that regard. God was so grieved by all the violence that resulted in humans killing each other, He wanted to make sure Noah and his family understood and would not allow it to happen again when they repopulated the earth.

Another important point: Ever wonder why Noah pleased God? The Bible uses the term, "found favor in the eyes of the Lord."[3] I would suggest that it was because Noah believed God. After all, he believed God when He said He was going to destroy the earth with a flood and then he spent about one hundred years building the ark and did exactly what God said to do. He did this despite any ridicule he may have received from the wicked people all those years around him who couldn't have missed seeing the large structure Noah was building and asked Noah what he was doing.

The Bible does not say Noah was perfect. However, it does imply that he believed God enough to obey Him, unlike Noah's ancestors Adam and Eve. That seems to be a theme we keep finding in the Bible. Believing God enough to do what He says regardless of what others may think about you seems to be pretty important to God. It seems like it is the dividing line between good and evil.

Why did God send the flood? To destroy wickedness. Why? Because wickedness results in violence and violence hurts God's creation, and specifically people. Because God loves people, the violence was breaking His heart.

God made people, and He called them good, yet they were destroying each other in wickedness and violence. God grieved over that, and still grieves today, like you would if somebody burned down your home.

However, Noah walked with God and believed Him, and God saved Noah and his family. We are learning more about God and understanding Him better. Let's keep going!

CHAPTER 3
GENESIS 11: FILL THE EARTH

Years ago, I received a phone call from the father of a Japanese foreign exchange student who was living with us then. Unfortunately, she was not there to take the call. I knew only one Japanese word, and it was the Japanese word for "hello". Her father appeared to know only one word of English, and it was "hello". We basically said "hello" to each other in the other person's language, back and forth, much like a game of ping pong.

I mentioned her name so that at least helped him to know he had not reached a wrong number. He couldn't tell me that he wanted to speak with his daughter, but I could figure that out just by the fact that he called. I couldn't tell him that his daughter was not home to take his call. I don't know if he figured that out or just thought that there was a crazy American custom of saying "hello" in someone else's language for several minutes before giving up the phone to the person for which the call was intended.

In a valiant effort to somehow convey what we were thinking to each other, we both resorted to saying "hello" slightly differently, with more emphasis on the first syllable, and then the second, or adding her name before or after "hello." Finally, after about five minutes of this back and forth, he gave up and hung up, probably thinking that he paid a lot of money for an international call to say "hello" with someone he didn't know.

With that phone conversation in mind, we come to Genesis 11 and the story of the Tower of Babel. This is another story where God's actions can appear to be mean. However, with a little thought and added perspective, we can get a better idea why God intervened like He did and understand Him better.

I have been a prankster at times in my life, so there have been times where I have purposely caused someone confusion and frustration for a brief amount of time in order to get a good laugh. None of them come close to the confusion and frustration that would be caused by changing the language of people who once knew the same language. If God were trying to play a practical joke on people, this would be the ultimate!

In reading Genesis 11, we see God was not playing a practical joke. Humankind was deliberately rebelling against God and disobeying His instructions to fill the earth. They had decided to stick together on a plain in the land of Shinar. Verse 4 shows their pride and contrary attitude, "Come, let us build ourselves a city and a tower with its top in the heavens, and let us make a name for ourselves, lest we be dispersed over the face of the whole earth." Like any parent, when children refuse to obey what they have been told, God found another way to get them to do what He wanted.

Depending on your viewpoint of God, you may view God's actions to "disperse them over the face of all the earth" as heavy-handed and cruel. Why wouldn't God allow them to stay together in families, staying close together to help each other?

Like any parent, when children refuse to obey what they have been told, God found another way to get them to do what He wanted.

Just like any parent, God doesn't always explain Himself. The Bible doesn't tell us the reason why He wanted humankind to disperse.

But after reading the first ten chapters of Genesis, I have some possibilities to offer:

First, it's possible God had created many good things in the earth for them to find. Forcing them to speak in different languages created a language barrier and dispersed them throughout the earth. If they just stayed in one part of the earth, all the wonderful things He created would remain undiscovered.

Picture an Easter egg hunt. As a parent, I have had the pleasure of hiding the eggs all over the yard. When my kids were very young, sometimes they would be scared and wouldn't want to venture too far. I would have to coax them to venture out further than they normally would be comfortable in order for them to find all the goodies that I had hidden for them to find.

My wife and I spent hundreds of hours finishing a room in our basement to make a playroom for our first grandchild (and for those that would come after her). We even built a playhouse with a reading loft, windows and even a working doorbell. When we first introduced the room to our granddaughter, we wanted her to explore the whole room and go find all the neat things we did for her. However, to our disappointment she tended to play near the door with some of her old toys.

In the same way, God has hidden many treasures throughout the whole earth that He created for our use and enjoyment. If humankind had been allowed to stay together where they were comfortable rather than disperse, we might not know today what cocoa beans, sugar cane and coffee beans are. We might not have some of the precious metals and materials we have today. That would mean a much less enjoyable life today in the lives of many people! Remember Proverbs 25:2, "It is the glory of God to conceal things, but the glory of kings is to search things out."

A second possibility for why God wanted them to disperse is that He wanted to protect them from each other. He had just destroyed all above-water life on the earth with a flood due to the amount of wickedness and murder going on in the earth. Perhaps

God was concerned they would start becoming violent again and by dispersing everyone over the earth, it would keep them apart and make murder much less likely.

A third possibility is that God wanted to protect them from His enemy, who has the name "Satan." While there was no longer the possibility for them to eat from the tree of life, there still existed the possibility that they could learn some horrible things from Satan. By having them disperse, any horrible effects that they might experience as a result of listening to Satan rather than God could be isolated rather than affecting all humankind again.

A fourth possibility is that by separating them to all the ends of the earth and giving them different languages, it would be much more difficult for the gospel (good news about Jesus) to be spread to all people. On the surface, this sounds like a horrible idea. However, if all the people of the world heard the gospel even with all the difficulty involved, it would then be obvious that it must have been something that God helped us do and not something we could have done by ourselves.

I wonder if God allows difficulties such as these to exist so that we realize it is only with His help that the difficulties can be overcome. It causes us to seek Him for help and creates more intimacy between Him and us when we come to Him for help. In creating and allowing difficulties like these, the goal is not to make our life difficult or miserable, but rather to bring us closer and increase our intimacy with Him.

There is no real way to know why God wanted them to disperse. Whatever the reason, it was for our good and not for our harm, and not because God is mean. A Bible verse that supports this thought is Deuteronomy 4:40 (italics added for emphasis): "Therefore you shall keep his statutes and his commandments, which I command you today, *that it may go well with you and with your children after you*, and that you may prolong your days in the land that the Lord your God is giving you for all time." Just like a loving parent, God gives us commands to "do this" or "don't do that" in order for things to go well for us. Sometimes, when we don't obey Him, He gets involved and causes circumstances to force us to do what we need to do, like what happened in Genesis 11.

Imagine: what if instead of congregating on the plain of Shinar, humankind would have dispersed like God wanted them to? We would have discovered all the things God wanted us to find, yet we could all be speaking the same language today. I wouldn't have had a five-minute phone call years ago trying to say something more than "hello." What a different world this would be today!

Let's read on and learn some more about God.

CHAPTER 4
GENESIS 12–14:
BLESSED, BUT DO YOU KNOW IT?

Genesis 12 opens with the following powerful statement God spoke to Abram: "Go from your country and your kindred and your father's house to the land that I will show you. And I will make of you a great nation, and I will bless you and make your name great, so that you will be a blessing. I will bless those who bless you, and him who dishonors you I will curse, and in you all the families of the earth shall be blessed."[1]

In the above statement, God commands Abram to leave his family and familiar settings behind and to go to another land. Amazingly, this is like what God had earlier told everyone on Earth to do prior to the whole tower of Babel incident. It is also similar to what Jesus told His disciples to do in Matthew 28:19, "Go, and make disciples of all nations . . ." with the key word being "Go."

In addition to God's command to Abram to leave his land and family, God says He will bless Abram and make him a blessing to every family of the earth. I find it so amazing that God wants to bless people. God didn't just want to bless Abram, but God wanted to bless "all the families of the earth" through him. Not some, but all!

This characteristic about God is so often overlooked by us as we read through the Bible. God could have been indifferent to the welfare of humankind at this point and just stepped back to see what they would make of themselves, maybe see whether they all survive or not, or see how badly they mess things up again. He could have said something like, "Let's let things play out and let the fittest and strongest survive." However, that was not God's intent. God had a plan to bless everyone on the earth, and He had chosen Abram to play a big role in that plan. That plan would result in Jesus, the seed of Abram, taking upon Himself the punishment for our sin so we could be reunited to God and be blessed as a result. We will talk more about this later. But for now, let's not forget that God wants to bless "all the families of the earth."

You might be thinking, "If God wanted to bless all families of the earth in Genesis 12, then why does He later in Genesis 19 destroy the people of Sodom and Gomorrah?" That is a good question, and one we will address when we review Genesis 19. For now, I want to point out that despite the people of Sodom being called "wicked, great sinners against the Lord" in Genesis 13[2], God *blessed* them through Abraham rescuing them in Genesis 14.

In Genesis 14, we learn that the people of Sodom and Gomorrah had been taken captive and taken away from their homes by other people. When Abram learns about this, and that his nephew Lot has also been taken captive with them, Abram gathers all his people who have been trained in combat (318 people, according to Genesis 14:14) travels many miles and rescues them from their captors and returns the people of Sodom and Gomorrah, along with their possessions, to their respective cities.

Abram could have just rescued Lot and Lot's family, but Abram did more than that. He also rescued the people of Sodom and Gomorrah. What a blessing Abram had already become! Despite their great wickedness, God blessed the people of Sodom and Gomorrah through Abram and rescued them from a horrible fate of slavery or death. It would have been enough if Abram had just rescued them, but he also returned to them all their possessions that had been taken, except for what his men had eaten.

What can we conclude from this? God the Father wants to bless people. That is an important characteristic of God. He doesn't want to hurt people. He wants to bless people. He did this first by making us in His image and giving us all of creation to enjoy. Now, it was through Abram that God intended to bless people.

With all that said, do you realize that you are blessed?

As I write this chapter, it's Christmastime. We as a family have just exchanged Christmas gifts with one another. Hopefully, everyone got something they are excited about. But you don't always get the gifts that you want.

Isn't it crazy how gifts that would have made you happy at one point in your life no longer get you excited at all? Toys were great when you were a kid, but if you got the same toys as an adult, how would you feel about that? And now that you are an adult, you may appreciate getting the latest and greatest cooking device to cook faster and better with less cleanup, but if you had received that when you were five, how would that have gone over?

If we take a peek over into Genesis 15:2, we can see that Abram even felt that way with God. "But Abram replied, 'O Sovereign Lord, what good are all your blessings when I don't even have a son? Since you've given me no children, Eliezer of Damascus, a servant in my household, will inherit all my wealth.'[3] Here, Abram is experiencing the same thing that you and I may have felt when getting a gift. Abram is asking God what good are all His blessings if he has no son with whom to share them.

That raises the question, "Is being blessed relative?" In other words, does being blessed vary in our eyes based on our circumstances at the moment?

1. You might not think Abram was blessed because he didn't have the latest cell phone, microwave, car or even a washer

and dryer! Yet, God was his friend, had blessed him tremendously with much wealth and had defended him from other men several times.

2. A man who just came out of a building a few minutes before it collapsed may feel very blessed, even though he lost all his possessions. He realizes he was so close to dying and is grateful to be alive.

3. A man who seemingly has everything a man could want, including being a famous celebrity, may not feel blessed. He may even feel so desperately dissatisfied with life that he takes his own life.

The point I am trying to make here is that you could be tremendously blessed by God, and yet not know it or not believe it. One reason could be because of where you are in life; you may not appreciate the value of what you have been blessed with. You could be like a two-year old child who chooses a gift of a single lollipop instead of an envelope with ten $100 bills in it with which he or she could buy more than a thousand lollipops. In other words, you may not value the things that matter and value the things that don't.

Is it the fault of the gift giver or the gift receiver that the gift is not properly valued?

God is good. You are richly blessed. Do you know that? Do you value that? The promise of God given to Abram in Genesis 12 has been fulfilled. God has made Abram into a great nation. God has blessed Abram. God has made Abram's name great so that it is remembered with admiration even today almost 4,000 years later. God made him a blessing to others. God has blessed those who blessed him and cursed those who cursed Abram. And most of all, God has blessed all the people on the earth through Abram. Maybe you don't understand how yet and don't properly value this gift from God, but you will. Keep reading and looking for God to reveal more of His goodness to you as you learn more about Him. Learning about God is like opening a Christmas present!

CHAPTER 5
GENESIS 15: FEAR NOT!

Genesis 15 opens with God stating one of the most profound and important statements that we will ever hear: "Fear not." These two words have been told to numerous people throughout the Bible. "Fear not." Translated today, that would read as "Do not be afraid."

God or His angels have been recorded in the Bible speaking the words, "Fear not," "Do not fear," "Be not afraid" or "Do not be afraid" to Abram,[1] Hagar,[2] Isaac,[3] Jacob,[4] Joshua,[5] Gideon,[6] Elijah,[7] Daniel,[8] Jeremiah,[9] Ezekiel,[10] Zechariah,[11] Mary,[12] Joseph,[13] shepherds in the fields near Bethlehem,[14] women at the empty tomb,[15] the Apostle Paul,[16] and finally the disciple John.[17] This list doesn't include the many times Jesus told people not to fear in the four gospels.

Why do you think God has felt the need to tell so many people not to fear? Because we can fear just about anything. We can fear death, disease, unemployment, bankruptcy, famine, war, ghosts, climate change, stock market crashes, mistreatment by others, people in the house or apartment living next to you, the government, and on and on. We can even fear things that don't exist but are just in our imaginations or in the movies, like zombies, for example. There is even a fear of missing out, often referred to as "FOMO," which is not taking advantage of something that we should benefit from. You name it. If left to ourselves, we will come up with plenty of things to fear.

Abram had his fair share of things to fear:

- He had left his familiar land to go to the land of Canaan as God instructed him to do. He was surrounded by strangers in a strange land, living as an outsider among them, prime ingredients for living a life full of fear.
- He had a beautiful wife. Normally that would be considered a blessing, but Abram was so fearful that others would kill him to take Sarai away from him that he had instructed her to tell them that she was his sister and not his wife! This was not a lie as she was his half-sister. This is recorded as actually happening twice where she was taken by other men to become their wives. God came to Abram's and Sarai's defense to give her back to Abram, so Abram's fear was not unfounded. If it had not been for God getting involved, it could have turned ugly for Abram and Sarai.
- He was also aware that others envied him for how blessed he was with material possessions. He told the King of Sodom that he didn't want any of the possessions of the people of Sodom (they were in Abram's possession after he had rescued the people of Sodom) because he didn't want the King of Sodom saying that Abram was rich because of them.
- His servants had disputes with his neighbors. Much later in Genesis 21, Abram makes a treaty with Abimelek at Abimelek's request to guarantee that Abram would treat Abimelek and his descendants with kindness. This emboldens Abram to speak up about a well Abimelek's servants had taken forcibly from Abram's servants. If Abram had

felt comfortable living among his neighbors, he probably would have brought this matter up much earlier. Instead, he brings it up only after many years have gone by (in Genesis 21) when he sees the fear Abimelek is showing toward him in asking for a treaty.

These are just the circumstances that are recorded in the Bible. There were probably many others that were not recorded. There was no shortage of things Abram could fear.

When Abram set out to rescue Lot and the people of Sodom and Gomorrah from the army that had taken them captive, the Bible mentions Abram had 318 of his servants trained to fight. Why do you think Abram had trained them to fight? Because he was fearful and wise enough to prepare for a possible fight in the foreign land where he was living. So, the words in Genesis 15:1, "Do not be afraid, Abram, for I will protect you, and your reward will be great"[18] were not just a trite Middle Eastern greeting as God visits him. These words should have had enormous meaning to Abram. But those words would only matter to Abram if he believed God was able to follow through on what He had just told Abram. If Abram didn't believe God, then he would continue being afraid and doubt everything else God had told him.

• • •

It had been about 10 years since God told Abram to leave Haran and go to Canaan where God would make him into *a great nation*. It was several years after that when God told him that He would give all the land around him to him *and his descendants*. It was a stretch back then to believe that he and Sarai would have any descendants of their own given their age. Now, Abram is probably thinking it has been so long that there is no way he and Sarai have any chance to have children to fulfill God's promises. He is now near 85 and Sarai near 75!

As a result, Abram asks God "O Sovereign Lord, what good are all your blessings when I don't even have a son? Since you've given me no children, Eliezer of Damascus, a servant in my household, will inherit all my wealth. You have given me no descendants of my own, so one of my servants will be my heir."[19]

But here is God's amazing answer to Abram's question: "Then the Lord said to him, 'No, your servant will not be your heir, for you will have a son of your own who will be your heir.' Then the Lord took Abram outside and said to him, 'Look up into the sky and count the stars if you can. That's how many descendants you will have!'"[20]

At age 85 with a wife at age 75, God is promising Abram that not only will he have a son of his own who will be his heir, but also that his descendants will be as numerous as the stars in the sky. Wow! That is quite the promise for people that old!

What follows next is one of the major verses of the Bible. It is the subject of many of the Apostle Paul's letters and will be quoted numerous times in the New Testament. It is a statement about what is in Abram's heart and mind and, more importantly, God's response to that.

Genesis 15:6 reads, "And Abram believed the Lord, and the Lord counted him as righteous because of his faith."[21] God didn't count Abram as righteous because of anything that Abram had done. Abram believed what God told him. That is why God counted him as righteous.

Does that sound familiar? Remember Adam and Eve in the Garden? God said something to them too. They believed Him for a while, but they let somebody else talk them out of believing God. With Satan's help, they went from believing what God said to then doubting what God said and then taking action that was directly disobedient to what God had told them.

Remember Noah? God said something to Noah too. Unlike Adam and Eve, Noah believed what God said and took action to obey Him. Like Abram, Noah was also considered a righteous man in God's eyes.

Here in Genesis 15, we see that Abram believed God. This is so important, so let me say it again. He believed God! That's why he was counted as righteous in God's eyes. This is an important point that is woven throughout the entire Bible. *God wants us to believe Him.* This is a fundamental requirement if we want to have any relationship with God. Our belief in Him shows up in our thoughts and actions and determines whether God considers us righteous or not.

What God is showing us here may be foreign to many in today's world, who believe righteousness is something to be earned or acquired by "conformity to an abstract moral code,"[22] or doing so many good deeds. On the contrary, in the Bible righteousness is "faithfulness to a relationship"[23], and the first requirement of this relationship is a belief that causes trust.

In only reading the first 15 chapters of the Bible, we have identified the epic battle of the universe in the eyes of God as recorded in the Bible. That battle is whether we will believe God enough to act accordingly. There is a great spiritual war that is taking place all centered around this one thing: Will we believe God enough to act on that belief?

> **There is a great spiritual war that is taking place all centered around this one thing: Will we believe God enough to act on that belief?**

As we read more of the Bible, we see that those who believe God and act accordingly are praised by God and reap His blessings. Those who don't are scolded by God and reap His punishment. Just like Adam and Eve, Noah, Abram and Sarai, and all the other people mentioned throughout the Bible, we of the 21st century are also in this spiritual war. Will we believe God? Will we obey Him because we believe Him? Which side of the war will we choose?

Action follows our beliefs. It's amazing how what we believe drives what we do and how we act. For example, if we believe God answers prayer, we will probably pray a lot. If we don't believe God will answer prayer, then we probably won't pray much, or we will pray only because we feel like we should or when other people are watching.

We probably won't pray when only God is watching. If we believe God wants us to help other people, we probably try to help other people. If we believe God doesn't care about other people, we probably don't help other people as much. What I heard recently says it well, "We may not believe what we profess, but we will live what we believe." (Dr. William E. Brown, PhD, August 5, 2019)

It can be easy to believe God when nothing major is at stake or there is no adversity for believing. But consider how there are bigger leagues for those who play sports like football, basketball and soccer. When these players become more skillful, they move up to junior varsity, then high school varsity, then college, then finally pro. So it is with those who enter the "contest" of either believing God or disbelieving God. As a person moves up to the bigger leagues, the opposition keeps getting tougher and tougher.

This is the contest that all of life is about. Will we fall short and stop believing? Or will we do what it takes to keep our belief and obey, regardless of the amount of opposition we face?

While believing God pleases God, it frustrates God's enemy. As with any war, the stakes are very high, and just about anything goes. If Satan can't talk you out of believing what God has said, he might try to force you to do so by bringing great suffering and even persecution to you. There are many stories later in the Bible of people who must suffer greatly in order to keep their belief in God. The Apostle Paul wrote that those who believed God enough to act accordingly would have to suffer persecution in order to keep that belief in Him.[24] This is still the case today.

Cole Richards, President of The Voice of the Martyrs, a ministry whose mission is to serve persecuted Christians through practical and spiritual assistance, recently wrote the following:

> Richard Wurmbrand [founder of The Voice of the Martyrs] often wrote sympathetically about Christians in Communist prisons who had buckled under horrific torture and denied Christ. In a Communist jail called Piteshti, the chief torturer, named Turcanu,

told Christians, "None of you will die as a martyr and go to heaven. We will make you blaspheme God and betray believers before dying to be sure you go to hell." Persecutors, like Turcanu, often try to make us apostates rather than martyrs. The enemy wants to bring dishonor to God and His gospel by showing our faith to be uncertain, weak or altogether false. The enemy whispers in our ears, "Must you always bear His shame?" Yes! And it is an honor to do so. Let's trust God for the strength and grace to boldly and passionately speak of His love and truth. He will empower us, and He will restore us when we fail. And let us pray that our persecuted brothers and sisters who endure torture and hardship for the name of Christ will also be strengthened when they face temptations to deny Him.[25]

Let's go back to the first part of Genesis 15 again where God told Abram "Fear not." God didn't remove all the things from Abram's life that may have caused Abram to fear. The strange people that he lived around still surrounded him. Sarai was still beautiful, and men would want her for their own at the risk of Abram's life (this happens again in Genesis 20). For Abram to "fear not," he had to decide to believe God despite the things around him. And if we want to believe God, we may have to believe God in spite of some scary things around us. Contrary to popular belief, whether or not we will believe God has a lot less to do with the external things that are around us and much more to do with what is in our head and what is in our heart.

I have lived in Kansas all my life. We have some amazing thunderstorms here. When I was a young child about 10 years old, I used to get so scared when the thunder from those storms not only woke me up but seemed to shake the entire house. Before the thunder hit, the sky would flash so bright from the lightning through the windows and light up the entire room. I would lie there in bed and see the flash of lightning. I knew the thunder was coming shortly after it. I would fear it so. Then one day I was reading something in the Bible that caught my attention and changed my perspective.

Jesus had sent out 72 disciples to preach the gospel in the various towns of Israel. When they returned to Jesus, they were full of joy saying, "Lord, even the demons are subject to us in your name!"[26] It was Jesus's reply to them that changed things for me. He said, "I saw Satan fall like lightning from heaven."[27] After thinking about that for a while, I went from fearing the thunder to cheering it. I pictured Satan falling from heaven because of Jesus's name being preached and lives being changed for good. I began to view the lightning and thunder as a positive event instead of a negative one. From that point forward, instead of trying to hide under the covers fearing the house was going to fall in, I envisioned someone accepting Christ or being healed and Satan getting kicked out of heaven. Did God change anything around me in order to free me from my fear? No. He simply changed what was between my ears and between my shoulders.

> **He simply changed what was between my ears and between my shoulders.**

Here are several favorite Bible passages of mine dealing with fear. I won't comment on them, but just let them speak to your heart and mind:

- "God is our refuge and strength, always ready to help in times of trouble. So we will not fear when earthquakes come and the mountains crumble into the sea. Let the oceans roar and foam. Let the mountains tremble as the waters surge!" (Psalm 46:1–3, NLT)
- "For God has not given us a spirit of fear and timidity, but of power, love, and self-discipline." (2 Timothy 1:7, NLT)
- "Such [God's] love has no fear, because perfect love expels all fear. If we are afraid, it is for fear of punishment, and this shows that we have not fully experienced his perfect love. We love each other because he loved us first." (I John 4:18–19, NLT)
- "I prayed to the Lord, and he answered me. He freed me from all my fears." (Psalm 34:4, NLT)

GENESIS 15: FEAR NOT!

- "So we can say with confidence, 'The Lord is my helper, so I will have no fear. What can mere people do to me?'" (Hebrews 13:6, NLT)
- "They do not fear bad news; they confidently trust the Lord to care for them." (Psalm 112:7, NLT)

God and Abram engage in an interesting interaction in the second part of Genesis 15. God chose to do something that in my mind demonstrates He is trying to get down to Abram's level, like a good father or mother bends down to talk to their young children at their level and in words their children can understand.

Verse 18 states God made a covenant with Abram to give his descendants the land. In those days, when you entered a covenant with someone, you sometimes would split an animal(s) in two, walking between them, pointing at them and stating, "May it be so done to me if I do not keep my oath and pledge."[28] I believe Abram realized that God was going to "cut covenant" with him when God told him in verses 9 and 10 to bring animals. Abram "cut them in two and arranged the halves opposite each other."[29] He had probably seen it or heard of it being done before and knew what was going to take place.

Abram prepares the animals and waits, a series of actions that Abram would only have done if he believed God. He did. God then shows up as a "smoking firepot with a blazing torch"[30] to put Himself under a curse if He did not keep the covenant with Abram.

Wow! Does that sound like an uncaring and distant God to you? God is God, so He can communicate however He wants. He chooses to reach out to Abram in such a way that Abram could understand completely based on Abram's experience and the customs of that age.

We've learned some big things in this chapter about our God:

1. People throughout history have struggled with fear and with not believing God. Like so many others who lived before us, God wants us to "fear not."

2. It is important to God that we believe Him. It is a theme mentioned throughout the entire Bible. Trust and belief that the other person in a relationship will keep their word is an important element of any good relationship, and very important in a relationship with God. Just like you would probably be offended if the people you valued in your life don't believe what you tell them, so God is offended when we, who were created in His image and to be in a loving and trusting relationship with Him, won't believe what He says.
3. Sometimes, the greatest obstacle to our believing God is in our own head and heart. At other times, there will be external opposition through life in general or through the enemy that will try to make it harder for us to keep believing God. God may remove that opposition, or He may allow it to remain in place for a season, so that we can learn to trust Him even in the face of great opposition.

Fear not! Believe God! Act accordingly!

CHAPTER 6
GENESIS 16: GOD ALWAYS SEES ME

Abram's wife Sarai had heard Abram share with her for years that God was going to make him into a great nation[1] and that God was going to give this faraway land that they had traveled to a decade ago to Abram's offspring.[2] A few years later, after Lot and Abram separated when they came back from Egypt, God told Abram again that He was going to give Abram's offspring all the land that he could see in every direction.[3] However, this time He added a new detail that his offspring would be so numerous that they would be impossible to count.[4] Abram undoubtedly shared this joyous news with his wife Sarai as well. Now, God had just talked with Abram and said those things again, and this time added another detail, that his heir will be a son coming from his own body.[5]

Can you imagine what Sarai must have felt at this great news? Pressure! Stress! Responsibility! Sarai could be thinking to herself, "Abram's promises from God could be fulfilled by now if it weren't for me. I can't seem to have children. It seems like God doesn't realize that when He is talking with Abram, that Abram is married to me, a woman who can't have children!" This is only my speculation, but it seems plausible based on the Bible text.

Back in those days, distractions to help you hide pain like TV, radio, computer games and social media didn't exist. As Sarai would sit in her tent to hide from the scorching sun, she would have lots of time, and maybe too much time to think and dwell on God's promises to Abram of having so many descendants that they can't be counted. These promises of God originally brought them joy. Now, these same promises seemed so cruel to Sarai as time and more time had gone by with her still not being able to become pregnant. God's promises were intended to be a blessing, but just the mention of them now painfully reminded Sarai of her inability to do what other women could do. Oh, how her heart must have hurt!

Sarai loved Abram and she wanted to see him receive these promises from God. And Abram loved Sarai. This is evident by the fact that he is in his mid-80s, very wealthy and had not taken another wife by now as other men at that time and in that culture did. He could have easily done so if he had any desire for anyone other than Sarai. Men in that day would have more than one wife just because they could if they could provide for them. But not Abram. He loved Sarai so much. Sarai was enough for him.

While Sarai was glad she was so loved by Abram and was his only wife, there were these promises of God that God had given Abram that needed to be fulfilled. Sarai was more than willing to do her part by having a baby. But while her mind was willing, her body was not cooperating. She tells Abram, "the Lord has prevented me from bearing children"[6] showing that at this point, she had given up on being able to conceive. Like us in difficult times, Sarai had further concluded that God must be actively involved in keeping her from having children. In other words, it's God's will. Or even, it's God's fault.

Sarai soon also concluded it would take the pressure from her if Abram had another wife through which God's promises to Abram could be fulfilled. She might have reasoned that it was God's desire in the first place for Abram to have another wife. After all, God had blessed Abram in so many other ways, why not bless him with another wife? It appears Abram wasn't ever going to suggest it. Time was running out, and someone must take action. So, Sarai does. She talks with Abram about giving Hagar, her servant, to be another wife to Abram so Abram can have children through her and then they can see God's promises fulfilled, at last. Abram agrees to Sarai's idea. He too wanted to have God's promises come true. Sarai's idea would do that.

A married couple having a child through a servant was not unheard of in their culture. It was repeated two generations later between Rachel and Jacob.[7] Approximately 1,900 years before the birth of Christ, culture was significantly different than what it is today. Back then, there were no government social programs to provide financial support for you in your old age or if you were hurt and couldn't work anymore. Children, male children especially, were the only means of provision for you in your old age.

So, they execute the plan and it works! Hagar becomes pregnant by Abram, and it looks like Abram is going to finally get his son that God has promised. But even the best man-made plans don't always work out so well. In this case, Hagar, who has been a servant of Sarai for some time, does something that her mistress Sarai can't do . . . become pregnant by Abram. This happens relatively quickly too. Apparently, this leads Hagar into feeling arrogant and she begins to despise Sarai. Perhaps Hagar was resentful about how all this happened and that she had no choice in the matter. We don't know. Regardless, Sarai feels the difference in Hagar's attitude toward her. Sarai tries to assert herself and put Hagar back in her place as her servant and a battle between them begins. Sarai then mistreats Hagar, and Hagar runs away.

This could have ended very badly for a lot of reasons. A pregnant Egyptian servant by herself in a strange, unfriendly, desert area is not a good situation. Fortunately, God intervenes as "the angel of the Lord."

While the text uses the term "the angel of the Lord", this may be one of those times in the Old Testament where it was really God Himself who was talking with her. This same thing happened to Moses, Joshua and several other people recorded in the Old Testament. With Moses in Exodus 3:2, the person is also described as the "angel of the Lord" but later says, "I am the God of your father, the God of Abraham, the God of Isaac, and the God of Jacob."[8] With Joshua, the text says Joshua saw a man who says He is the "Commander of the army of the Lord."[9] Joshua quickly bows before Him in worship and the man tells Joshua to take off his shoes because he is standing on holy ground, just like God told Moses at the burning bush. That's why I and many scholars believe this was an Old Testament appearance of Jesus to Hagar. Jesus existed as God with His Father before the Christmas story ever took place and that is why people saw Him in the Old Testament.

God interrupts the silence of the desert by saying, "Hagar, servant of Sarai." This must have scared Hagar because she thought she was alone. Here was someone she didn't know, but He certainly knew her. He knew her name and that she was Sarai's servant. Who told Him? He then tells her to return to Sarai and submit to her. He adds, "I will surely multiply your offspring so that they cannot be numbered for multitude. Behold, you are pregnant and shall bear a son. You shall call his name Ishmael, because the Lord has listened to your affliction."[10] God says more but it is about Hagar's son's future rather than about God seeing and listening to her.

Hagar returns to Sarai and Abram and tells them what she was told by God. God has made such a favorable impression on her. She says about the Lord who spoke to her, "You are a God of seeing. Truly here I have seen Him who looks after me." While Hagar was thinking she was all by herself, both in terms of being all alone in the desert, and in terms of no one else caring for her, God has shown her that He sees her, is looking after her and cares about her so much to come to her in a desert place.

GENESIS 16: GOD ALWAYS SEES ME 49

I also find it interesting that God tells her that He has listened to her affliction. Wow! He has seen and heard all that she has gone through with Sarai. And maybe there was more in Hagar's heart that God heard from her in that place than just her mistreatment from Sarai. Maybe also the unfortunate events Hagar experienced in becoming a servant in the first place? Maybe there were other hurts in Hagar's past that contributed to her decision to flee and run into the desert to get away from it all? Regardless, God showed up.

Note that He didn't tell her what she wanted to hear. He didn't help her have a fine pity party. Rather, He told her to return to Sarai and submit to her. He didn't justify Sarai's actions and ignore the mistreatment, but He did call out Hagar for her part in things and told her to submit to Sarai. But that was okay for Hagar because God showed her she was significant to Him. He had listened to her affliction and He saw her.

Perhaps you are reading this, and you have children of your own. Or you are a supervisor at work and have employees working for you. Be aware that it is very important that those under your authority feel that you have heard them. That doesn't mean you must agree with them or do what they ask, but you need to listen to them so that they know they have been heard. **Do you want to make someone feel loved? Listen to them well.** Look what it did for Hagar.

I tend to give more validity to what God says about Himself in the Bible compared to the things people say about God. That's because what people say about God can be flawed, and the Bible can be simply recording what they say about God rather than stating a fact about God. However, what Hagar says about God here agrees with what scripture says elsewhere and is right on. God sees us! Always!

One of my favorite verses states, "I could ask the darkness to hide me and the light around me to become night but even in darkness I cannot hide from you. To you the night shines as bright as day. Darkness and light are the same to you."[11] Yes, God can see in the dark. In fact, light was the first thing that God created in the Genesis account of creation.[12] God was doing quite well without light before He created light. So, rather than saying God can see in the dark, I should instead say that God can always see, period.

Another favorite verse of mine paints a picture of God not just looking, but aggressively searching the earth for those who want God in their lives. "For the eyes of the Lord search back and forth across the whole earth, looking for people whose hearts are perfect toward him, so that he can show his great power in helping them."[13] As I picture it, He is not just out and about passively walking on a relaxing stroll and just happens upon us by accident. He didn't just coincidentally come across Hagar during His daily stroll. Instead, He is running, like a child at an Easter egg hunt, looking for those who have turned their hearts toward Him!

Whether there is light, darkness, distance, time, stress, anger or any other variable involved, God sees you. Paul says it best in Romans 8:38–39, "For I am sure that neither death nor life, nor angels nor rulers, nor things present nor things to come, nor powers, nor height nor depth, nor anything else in all creation, will be able to separate us from the love of God in Christ Jesus our Lord."[14]

To conclude this chapter, let me encourage you. You may feel hopeless and abandoned. You may feel invisible, oblivious to others. But God sees you and is looking after you. If you will believe Him and submit to His direction, He can lead you out of the desert you are experiencing just like He did with Hagar. Just don't get impatient with Him. Hagar had to retrace all of her steps to return from the desert that she had run into trying to get away. It may take you some time to walk back out of the desert that you have run into when you tried to get away from your circumstances. Believe Him. Trust Him. Submit to Him. Do what He directs and walk out of your desert. And remember that He is watching you all the way with eyes that care for you.

CHAPTER 7
GENESIS 17: ONE STEP AT A TIME

Have you ever wondered why God seems to share just little bits of information with you and doesn't share all the details of His plans? I certainly have. I have prayed many times that God would show me the specifics of what His will is for me in a specific situation, so I can go out and do what I think He wants. Rarely do I get that direction right away, and usually it seems as though I don't get an answer at all. It feels like He doesn't want to share those things with me.

I have had people tell me that I need to be patient and wait on God. They quote Bible verses to me like Habakkuk 2:3, "But these things I plan won't happen right away. Slowly, steadily, surely, the time approaches when the vision will be fulfilled. If it seems slow, do not despair, for these things will surely come to pass. Just be patient! They will not be overdue a single day!"[1] I appreciate what they are telling me. Sometimes, though, it can be hard for me to wait, especially when I don't have the ability to see the details of what I am waiting for.

I remember when growing up my mom quoted to me a few times Psalm 119:105, "Thy word is a lamp unto my feet, and a light unto my path."[2] She then explained that God didn't promise to give us direction for our entire life today, but just one step at a time. Just like a person holding a lantern at night can only see one and maybe two steps in front of them, so the Lord will give us direction, but usually that is only one step in front of us at a time. Therefore, I shouldn't be impatient but just keep taking the one step in front of me that I feel the Lord leading me and He will guide me down the entire path of my life. My mom's counsel has helped me many times over the years. But when you are at a fork in the road of your life and want to choose the right path, it's hard to trust and wait.

Have you ever felt this way or am I the only one?

After re-reading about Abram and Sarai up through Genesis 16, and now reading the first part of Genesis 17, I think I am starting to see something that helps me somewhat better understand why God only shares one step at a time with me.

Let's take a step back in time and look at what God has told Abram so far about having descendants:[3]

1. Genesis 12:2, "I will *make of you a great nation.*"
2. Genesis 12:7, "To *your offspring* I will give this land."
3. Genesis 13:15–16, "... for all the land that you see I will give to you and to your offspring forever. I will make *your offspring as the dust of the earth*, so that if one can count the dust of the earth, your offspring also can be counted."
4. Genesis 15:4, "This man [Eliezer of Damascus] shall not be your heir; *your very own son shall be your heir.*" And he brought him outside and said, "Look toward heaven, and number the stars, if you are able to number them." Then he said to him, "So shall your offspring be."
5. Genesis 15:18, "To your offspring *I give this land, from the river of Egypt to the great river, the river Euphrates,* ..."

Did you notice that each time God speaks to Abram, He shares a little more information regarding His plans with Abram? It's similar to what my mom was telling me, the light of God's guidance only reaches one stone in front of you.

Now, we are in Genesis 17. It has been about 15 years since a conversation between God and Abram had been recorded. The last conversation was the conversation recorded in Genesis 15:18, and Abram was probably 84 years old when that took place. Ishmael had not even been conceived at that point. Now, when Abram was now 99 years old and Ishmael was 13 years old, the Lord appears to Abram and shares a lot more information. Genesis 17:3–8 reads [italics added to show the new things God is sharing]:

> Then Abram fell on his face. And God said to him, "Behold, my covenant is with you, and you shall be the father of *a multitude of nations*. No longer shall your name be called Abram, but *your name shall be Abraham, for I have made you the father of a multitude of nations*. I will make you exceedingly fruitful, and I will make you into nations, and *kings shall come from you*. And I will establish my covenant between me and you *and your offspring after you throughout their generations for an everlasting covenant*, to be God to you *and to your offspring after you*. And I will give to you and to your offspring after you the land of your sojournings, all the land of Canaan, for an everlasting possession, *and I will be their God*."

Abram now learns that:

1. He will be father of a multitude of nations, not just one.
2. His name is changed to Abraham to reflect this.
3. Kings will come from him.
4. God will now include Abraham's offspring in their covenant, making it an "everlasting" covenant.
5. God will be the God of Abraham's offspring too.

Wow! What fantastic news! God could have ended there. In fact, Abraham probably expected God to stop there. This is more information than God has ever shared with Abraham. Abraham is excited that all of this is going to be fulfilled, but I believe he misunderstood and thought it would be fulfilled through his son Ishmael. Oh, what a blessing Ishmael has become, he thinks!

God then even shares more! In a nutshell, God explains that the covenant between God and Abraham will be recognized by the circumcision of every male. Every male in Abraham's house, whether born free or bought with money, can accept the covenant if they are circumcised in their foreskin. If they refuse circumcision, then they are excluded from the covenant. It's their choice to be included or excluded.

It is my understanding that women at that time were considered joined to their father or their husband, so if their father or husband were in the covenant, they were too.

God is now going to say something to Abraham about Sarai. There is no recorded conversation to this point between God and Abraham about Sarai. Genesis 17:15–21 reads as:

> And God said to Abraham, "As for Sarai your wife, you shall not call her name Sarai, but Sarah shall be her name. I will bless her, and moreover, I will give you a son by her. I will bless her, and she shall become nations; kings of peoples shall come from her." Then Abraham fell on his face and laughed and said to himself, "Shall a child be born to a man who is a hundred years old? Shall Sarah, who is ninety years old, bear a child?" And Abraham said to God, "Oh that Ishmael might live before you!" God said, "No, but Sarah your wife shall bear you a son, and you shall call his name Isaac. I will establish my covenant with him as an everlasting covenant for his offspring after him. As for Ishmael, I have heard you; behold, I have blessed him and will make him fruitful and multiply him greatly. He shall father twelve princes, and I will

make him into a great nation. But I will establish my covenant with Isaac, whom Sarah shall bear to you at this time next year."

Wow! What news! Not only is God going to make Abraham a father of nations, but He is also saying that this will happen through Sarai, whose name has now been changed to Sarah to reflect this, because she will be a mother of nations! And they are to call her son Isaac.

God wanted to eliminate any chance that Abraham could think that he misheard or misunderstood God and still believe that through Hagar and Ishmael the promises from God would be fulfilled. So, He repeated Himself and said it again. It was through a child born to Sarah that God would fulfill His promises to Abraham.

I noticed something in this conversation God had with Abraham that I like about God. Note that at first Abraham couldn't wrap his head around Ishmael not being his son of promise and so he attempts to help God out by saying, "Oh that Ishmael might live before you!" God didn't chastise him for unbelief but seemed to understand that Abraham might not be able to wrap his mind around what He had just told Abraham. So, God corrects Abraham graciously and speaks in a way that Abraham can understand clearly. From that point, Abraham believes God fully. Abraham even goes out and circumcises himself and all the males in his house that very day. Once again, he believed God to the point where he acted completely in obedience to God.

Sometimes we get in our head pictures of God much like Dorothy had of the Wizard of Oz before Toto pulled open the curtain on the wizard. We picture flames shooting up and the wizard yelling. God could speak in a way that makes the Wizard of Oz's fury look like that of a harmless flea if He wanted. But that is not usually how God speaks to us; He rarely acts that way.

A story that supports that is when the prophet Elijah went to Mount Sinai to seek God, the Lord passed by the cave he was in. This caused a mighty blast of wind to hit the mountain that tore loose some of the rock. After the wind, there was an earthquake, and after the earthquake was a fire. As powerful as those must have seemed, the Bible says that the Lord was not in any of them. Maybe that's why Elijah stayed where he was at that moment. But then came a "still small voice,"[4] a "gentle whisper,"[5] and when Elijah heard it, he wrapped his face and went out to the entrance to talk with the Lord. He perceived God's presence in the still small voice and responded to it rather than the powerful things he saw and heard.[6]

Imagine that! The Creator of the universe speaking in a whisper. For you to hear a whisper, you have to be close or get close to the person whispering to hear them. That's why God often speaks in a whisper, to encourage you to stop, be still and listen; to seek him and get close to him. He loves you and his goal is closeness with you.[7]

> **God often speaks in a whisper, to encourage you to stop, be still and listen**

Now I wonder what Sarah thought when Abraham told her about this conversation. Maybe he didn't tell her and was afraid to tell her based on the past series of events with Hagar and Ishmael? Note that in Genesis 18 when God comes to visit Abraham and Sarah with two angels also in the form of men, they ask where Sarah is. Then they say that about a year from now, Sarah will have a son. Note that Abraham didn't laugh this time, but Sarah did, like Abraham did the first time that he heard God tell him back in Genesis 17. That's why I wonder if Abraham didn't tell Sarah that God had told him that she was going to have a son and that God telling her this news was the first time she had heard it. I wonder if one reason God came on the scene in Genesis 18 was to give Sarah a chance to hear the news and believe before Sarah's body began changing to either become pregnant or as a result of being pregnant.

While Sarah could be admired for being so selfless in giving her servant Hagar to Abraham so that Abraham could have a son, things did not work out as she and Abraham had thought. Her and Abraham's plans to help bring to pass God's promises actually ended up getting in the way. Both Abraham and Sarah had now discovered that God intended to do "far more abundantly than all that we ask or think."[8] They found out God doesn't need help fulfilling His promises, and that it is better to wait on God.

If you are like me, you're probably wondering if Sarah giving Hagar to Abraham was a mistake made by Abraham and Sarah or if it was God's plan. I think it was a mistake, but I don't believe there is any way this side of heaven to know one way or the other. However, even if Ishmael's birth was not God's original plan, I don't believe there is any such thing as a mistake when it comes to the conception of a child. God could have intervened if it was going to mess up His plans. You know, as I get older in the Lord, I believe there is nothing that can mess up the plans of God. There is nothing that catches Him by surprise. I cannot picture God saying to Himself, "Oh no! I didn't think that they would do that! What am I going to do now?!"

A friend of mine used the term, "Crazy Quilter" to refer to herself recently after I had mentioned to her that she was good at dealing with obstacles that arise suddenly. When I asked her what the term meant, she said that while making a quilt, she will suddenly see a piece of fabric that was not in her plan that she will include as she goes.

In the same way, I think God would be a great "Crazy Quilter." Nothing takes Him by surprise. I'm not saying He will be pleased with whatever we do. He has told us plainly the things that displease Him in His Word and we should strive not to offend Him by doing them. However, there isn't anything we can do that can mess Him up. Now, we may not like the way He "quilts" around our mistakes, or the consequences we suffer because of them, but as it affects Him, He can weave them into His overall plan for His kingdom without any problems. Romans 8:28, one of my favorite verses, speaks of this as it reads, "And we know that for those who love God all things work together for good, for those who are called according to his purpose." Note that the verse does not say that all things are good, but instead that all things work together for good for those who love God.

My wife used to do a lot of needlepoint and cross-stitch pictures years ago. We have a few of them that are framed and hanging in our house. In those days, I loved to lie on the floor in front of the chair that she would sit in to watch TV. Oh, how sweet the days of young love! When I would turn to look up at her, I would see what she was working on from my vantage point. Frankly, it didn't look very good from that perspective. Thread would be going in what appeared to be sporadic directions along the back of the fabric she was working on. There would be knots here and there where you could see she changed direction and changed threads. However, when I got up and looked at the other side she was seeing, it looked great. A beautiful picture was in progress of being made. I think the same goes with God and our lives. From my perspective here on earth, my life may seem disorganized and unplanned. There have been unexpected, unpleasant and sometimes dramatic changes in direction that make no sense to me here. However, I live my life by faith in God that someday, when I get to heaven and can see my life from His perspective, I won't see any of the imperfections that I see while here on earth. Instead, I trust I will see my life and the perfect picture that He has made it out to be from His heavenly vantage point.

From all of this, we can conclude:

1. God keeps secrets from us when it is best. If He shared everything with us, with that knowledge we would most likely, with the best of intentions, do things to mess up His plans. Therefore, He conceals things and reveals things to us as it seems best to Him. Remember the verse Proverbs 25:2 that I mentioned in the Introduction, "It is the glory of God to conceal things, but the glory of kings is to search things out."

2. Not everything that is recorded in the Bible was a result of God's actions. For example, even though it was done with good intentions, it was Sarah's idea to give Hagar to Abraham, but that was not God's way to have the promises fulfilled.

3. God can work out all things (mistakes, things people do to hurt us, and whatever else fits into the definition of "all") for the good of those who love Him: see Romans 8:28.
4. I need to trust my life's plan to God and be content to seeing one step at a time, walking in the light He gives me and following Him wherever He leads me; see Psalm 119:105.

Are you beginning to understand God more? I am. Let's keep going because there is so much more to understand in our quest to know Him.

CHAPTER 8
GENESIS 18: YOUR FATHER IS *THE* JUDGE

Can you recall the last time or two that you met someone new? In your first conversation with them, did they ask you what you did for a living? If you are currently in school, did they ask what you were hoping to do someday for a living? Did you ask them similar questions? Now try to recall why you think they asked you those types of questions or why you asked them. Was it out of courtesy or are we trying to get information to help us to know them better?

Once we understand what a person does or wants to do to earn a living, it may shed light on their personality and skills and what they are like. We must be careful though, because we can try to stereotype the person we've met based on what we think people of that occupation are like when they may be an exception to the rule, or the rule may not be legitimate.

For example, if I told you about a friend of mine who was a nurse, and you thought nurses were generally compassionate, caring and smart, you might assume my friend was also compassionate, caring and smart. In this case, I would agree with you. But, if you assumed my friend was female, I would not agree with you. My friend is a male.

But knowing my friend is a nurse would help you to understand whether he likely knows the medical names of parts of the human anatomy, works unusual hours, and other things particular to nurses. So, knowing a person's occupation could help you quickly learn more about a person and understand them better if you have an accurate understanding of the common traits of that occupation.

Did you know that God has an occupation? He is a Judge! Abraham in Genesis 18:25 referred to Him as such when he was talking with Him. Abraham says, "Shall not the Judge of all the earth do what is just?" Throughout the Bible you will see references to God as a judge. This is an important point and I want to stress it one more time to you because it will help you understand more of what God is doing in the Bible and in our own lives as well. Think of Him as Abraham did, as the "Judge of all the Earth."

What was your first reaction when I said in the paragraph above that God is a judge? Was it good? Was it bad? Was it even scary? Perhaps you already have had an experience where you were in court with a judge. In that case, especially if things didn't work out so well for you, you may have an unfavorable impression of anyone that is a judge. I can relate. I have had both good and bad experiences with judges. But for me to make a judgment that all judges are the same based on what I myself have experienced would be a mistake. That would be the equivalent of saying that all nurses are alike.

About 2,500 years ago, the Greek philosopher Socrates stated the following characteristics of a good judge: "To hear courteously, to answer wisely, to consider soberly, and to decide impartially."[1] I believe God demonstrates all four of these characteristics but I want to focus at the moment on the fourth characteristic Socrates mentioned, as I believe that is the one most people have difficulty with in understanding God.

An impartial judge must treat all parties in the courtroom the same. He or she can't be more sympathetic to one side or the other.

He or she can't cut someone some slack or give someone a break because in giving one party a break, he or she is taking something from the other party.

A judge in many ways is like a referee or an umpire in a sports game. Referees and umpires are also supposed to be impartial. The reason referee and umpire uniforms are black, or of some black and white combination, is to identify them as not being a participant in the game or in support of either team. They are not allowed to take the ball and shoot it for one of the teams they like. They must remain neutral to both teams competing.

I played baseball at an early age. I remember one of my very first games where my coach told me to run to second base. It was the last inning of the game and we already had two outs. I slid into second base because it was a close play, and the ball had been thrown to the second basemen in order to try to tag me out. I ran as fast as I could and made a perfect slide, but the second basemen caught the ball and put it quickly in front of second base just in time so that my foot slid into his glove.

The umpire at second base was a very nice man in town who had always spoken kindly to me around town. To my surprise, he yelled, "You're out!" He just didn't objectively and calmly state this fact. He yelled it, screaming it at the top of his lungs and gestured by emphatically throwing his right thumb high into the air so that there was no doubt about what he was saying. That ended the game. I was devastated. Not only by being the last out of the game, but in the manner this normally nice man called me out. But he was doing his job and doing it well. He couldn't deny that I had been tagged out because he knew me. He couldn't cut me some slack because we were from the same town and the other team was from a different town. He had to be fair to both teams, regardless of any affiliations between one team and himself. He had to do his job and do it in a manner that was impartial to both teams, making the calls and reacting as baseball umpires do so that no one would question his impartiality.

In the same way, God, if He is to be a just judge, must judge everyone with complete impartiality. He cannot cut someone a break just because they are rich, poor, smart, likeable, cute or possess any other human attributes that we feel could influence humans in making a judgment. If He, or any earthly judge would do so, they would not be totally impartial and would not be just. Consider this if you feel that God sometimes treats you differently than the beloved child that you are, and with ruthless impartiality. As much as He loves you, He must judge justly and impartially.

Here are some verses where the Bible refers to God being an impartial judge:

- "For God shows no partiality." (Romans 2:11)
- "And if you call on him as Father who judges impartially according to each one's deeds," (I Peter 1:17)
- "At the set time that I appoint, I [God] will judge with equity [impartiality]." (Psalm 75:2)

As we explore what it means for God to be a judge, we've learned that He will be impartial. Will He also be fair? I will try to answer that question by saying it depends on how you define "fair." If by being fair, you mean that God will apply the rules equally to everyone, I would say yes, He is fair. However, if you mean that He will try to equalize everyone by helping the poor or less fortunate at the expense of others, then I would say no, He won't be fair, but will judge rightly toward all. I say this based on what He told Moses to tell the Israelites, "Do not twist justice in legal matters by favoring the poor or being partial to the rich and powerful. Always judge people fairly."[2]

So, in our quest to better understand and know God, we've learned that He is the Judge over all the earth and, as such, judges righteously with impartiality and fairness. You may ask, "So what? How does that affect me?" A lot! Bear with me as I share more about an experience that I hope will open your eyes like it did mine.

I didn't have much of an understanding of what court was really like until a time when I had the opportunity to be a representative on behalf of a family member in a legal matter. This was a civil matter (dispute involving the rights of the parties) rather than a criminal matter (dispute involving possible violation of laws) because it pertained to someone else making a claim to the house that my family member owned and was living in at the time. The other parties were making a claim that my family member did not properly own the house and that it should be their property instead. The other parties hired a law firm and filed a claim against my family member with the court. Therefore, we also had to hire an attorney in order to defend her ownership of the house. Many documents were presented by the parties to be reviewed by the judge prior to us appearing in court. They and their attorney appeared in court, and to defend my family member against their claims, I and our attorney also had to appear in court. Then there was discussion and debate between the attorneys before the judge. We all then went home with the understanding that the judge would review the matter. A few days later we learned that the judge ruled in our favor, and our family member got to keep her house.

As I reviewed the documents, I found it so interesting that both our attorney and the other side's attorneys used the phrase, "We pray the court that . . ." numerous times throughout the documents. When they did so, the attorneys essentially were saying, "We ask the court to rule in our favor because . . ." Until then, I had never heard the word "pray" used in anything other than a spiritual context. I think it was seeing this language used, specifically the words, "pray the court" that opened my eyes to see that there are a lot of parallels between the American judicial court and the heavenly court in which our Heavenly Father presides as Judge. Let's walk through some of these similarities now as I believe it will give you a better understanding of God our Father, as well as the spiritual legal battle that we are involved in every day whether we know it or not.

In the case involving my family member, the other side was represented by an attorney who, while speaking truth, was speaking only the truth from their point of view that would help their case and hurt our arguments before the Judge. Fortunately, this was a civil case that we were involved in. If this had been a criminal case, the other side would have been a prosecuting attorney who would have been accusing us of specific wrongdoings that he or she wanted us to be found guilty of and punished with fines, imprisonment, or both. This image of a prosecuting attorney bringing accusations against someone in court reminds me of Satan, who the Bible refers to as the "accuser of our brother and sisters":

> The great dragon was hurled down—that ancient serpent called the devil, or Satan, who leads the whole world astray. He was hurled to the earth, and his angels with him. Then I heard a loud voice in heaven say: 'Now have come the salvation and the power and the kingdom of our God, and the authority of his Messiah. For the accuser of our brothers and sisters, who accuses them before our God day and night, has been hurled down. They triumphed over him by the blood of the Lamb and by the word of their testimony; they did not love their lives so much as to shrink from death.[3]

Did you catch that Satan is accusing us before God "day and night?" Unfortunately, he probably doesn't have to make up things to accuse us of. Even though Jesus called him not only a Liar, but the father of lies,[4] we probably give Satan enough negative material of us breaking God's laws "day and night" that he doesn't need to lie before our Heavenly Father, the Judge of all the Earth. The Bible does tell the story of a man named Job who was such a righteous man that Satan couldn't lay an accusation of wrong-doing on him, but that didn't keep Satan from trying to persuade God to allow him, to use a legal phrase, to "throw the book" at Job. Satan is so crafty and clever. He is one prosecuting attorney you wouldn't want to face in an earthly courtroom, let alone heavenly courtroom.

Now, if you are a prosecuting attorney or know of one, please accept my apologies for making a comparison between your role in court and what Satan is doing in the heavenly court. I'm sure you are just doing your job in presenting to the court the evidence that has been found against someone so that the laws of our countries are followed, and the rule of law prevails in our countries rather than a state of lawlessness, chaos and anarchy. But the comparison is too accurate and important for us not to use to explain things in the spirit.

Whereas a prosecuting attorney probably does not have a personal grudge against those whom they are trying to prosecute, the same cannot be said of Satan. Satan hates us with a passion:

- "Be careful—watch out for attacks from Satan, your great enemy. He prowls around like a hungry, roaring lion, looking for some victim to tear apart." (I Peter 5:8, TLB)
- "The thief [Satan] comes only to steal and kill and destroy. I [Jesus] came that they may have life and have it abundantly." (John 10:10)

You've probably heard of prosecuting attorneys trying to settle cases against defendants in order to save time and money for both sides in our courts. In our court system, this can be good for either or both parties and is done often. In the civil court matter involving a family member that I helped, the attorney for the other side tried to make a settlement offer with us, requesting a sum of money that we would pay them in order for them to give up their claim to the house. In order to convince you to take a settlement offer, the other party will make their case sound like they can't lose, that they've got you in a big predicament, and that the best thing for you to do is accept their offer. It may or may not be malicious. It depends on the motives of the other party and the facts of the case.

You can bet that Satan, your great enemy, is a master at getting people to settle with him out of court. First, he will try to convince you that God doesn't exist or that there is no way for you to know Him. He wants you to believe you are foolish to be thinking there is a God that might love you. If those arguments don't work, he will try to make you think you wouldn't like God at all; that God is mean, unfair, boring and just cares about a bunch of rules. Satan wants to eliminate any possibility that you would worry about your relationship with God and just enjoy your life. Satan wants you to settle, with you being resigned to live life without God in this life and in the life to come. By settling, you are agreeing that you are guilty and will pay whatever is the penalty.

Satan will also do his best to keep you from finding a good defense attorney to represent you. Abraham Lincoln has reportedly been quoted as saying, "He who represents himself has a fool for a client."[5] I think you would be a fool if you chose to represent yourself in the heavenly court. It would be one thing if you were truly innocent in every regard, but you are not. None of us are. The Bible is quite clear about that.[6] The punishment for any sin is death via eternal separation from God in the lake of fire.[7]

Fortunately, you don't have to represent yourself in the heavenly court. Jesus has offered to be your advocate and defend you. He has already agreed to represent you if you will ask Him to do so. Yet, no attorney wants a client that won't listen to him or her and do what they say. The same applies to Jesus.[8] For Him to be your defense attorney, you have to publicly declare that He is your only defense attorney,[9] confess your sins to Him so He can make your guilty plea,[10] and then trust Him enough to do everything that He tells you to do from that point forward.[11] While He will represent you for free, doing the things that He tells you to do may cost you a lot.[12] But if you do all these things, then He will not only represent you in the heavenly court, He has promised to pay the penalty for all of your sins Himself. Wow! How can you refuse such an opportunity?

Unfortunately, a lot of people miss out on this offer that Jesus has presented to them. They may:

- Think the offer is silly or too good to be true[13]
- Be ashamed if family or friends know they have put their trust in Jesus to represent them[14]

- Think the deal is a great deal, but don't like submitting to someone else and doing whatever they say[15]
- Think that there are many defense attorneys besides Jesus who will represent you, including paying your penalty[16]

For one reason or another, lots of people look into Jesus's offer, but decide to decline it or put it off to worry about another day, only to forget about it due to other pressing but much less important needs.[17] Do not be like them!

Why would Jesus do all of this for you? Because He obeyed God the Father.[18] You see, not only does Jesus love you, so does God the Father.[19] It was God the Father's idea[20] and is the only way that He can satisfy justice while also saving you from eternal punishment. While He loves you tremendously, God the Father just can't let you off the hook for all your sins. Think of the uproar from Satan and everyone else doomed to hell because of their sin accusing God of being partial and unjust by letting you off the hook. Even if God could keep it just between you and Him, that wouldn't work, because God would know. It is impossible for Him to sin by lying and overlooking justice like that.[21] God is not God if He is not faithful to judge impartially and righteously.

Having Jesus pay the penalty for you was the only way God could save you. Now, when Satan wants to accuse you to God day and night asking God to punish you, God can gladly reply, "Your motion is denied! Jesus, as creator of all humankind[22] and in whose image they were created,[23] suffered death for sin in their place.[24] This court has previously ruled that the death of the creator is sufficient payment for all sins of His creation. Therefore, any of them who accepts Jesus's representation and payment in the class action case brought before this court are recognized as being represented by Him. There is no more penalty for their sins remaining to be paid, and they have all rights and privileges afforded to them by their legal representative. Therefore, your motion is denied!"

Wow! And that's not all! Once the case is dismissed, court is over. God leaves the courtroom to go home, where He is throwing a party at His house to honor Jesus and those who trusted Him for representation. God considers those Jesus represents as family. It will last forever and will be heaven, literally. Be there! For more details on how to accept Jesus's offer of representation and payment of your penalty, and to follow what He says, see Appendix A.

Before we move on, there is one more very important point to make. Remember how we discussed that a judge must be completely impartial? That means he cannot act on the behalf of either side in a court case, even if he were a friend or relative. He cannot make a motion for them but can only respond to motions they make in court. He is the referee, not a participant. Therefore, if he would want something to be done for one of the parties in a court case, he has to rely on one of the two sides to request it of him as the judge.

With that in mind, I suggest to you that this is why Jesus so often encouraged us to ask things of God. To use a court term, that is why He encouraged us to "pray" to God. On one side of the heavenly courtroom we have Satan making requests of God "day and night," accusing us and demanding that we get justice for our sins. On the other side of the heavenly courtroom, we have Jesus and those He is representing.

A biblical example of this is when Jesus told Peter, "Satan has asked to sift all of you as wheat. But I have prayed for you, Simon, that your faith may not fail. And when you have turned back, strengthen your brothers."[25] This courtroom battle continues today. Satan and his team are on one side of the heavenly courtroom making requests of God (such as what Jesus told Peter about in our example), to sift you as wheat. I can only imagine some of the other requests that are being made, requests like:

- "God, how many times are you going to let him commit that sin and not reap the consequences for it? Galatians 6:7 says you will not be mocked and that whatever a man sows, that will he also reap. When are you going to allow us to make him reap what he has sown?"

- "God, he only loves and obeys You because you protect and bless him. Allow us to mess up some area of his life for just a short while and see how quickly he will turn away from You. You aren't really his God. Your blessings are his god! Separate Your blessing from Yourself and see which one he seeks after!"[26]

Fortunately, Jesus and His team are on the other side of the heavenly courtroom. You are part of that team if you have accepted Jesus's invitation to represent you and complying with the terms of that arrangement (see Appendix A). We too can be entering pleas made on the behalf and in the name of Jesus, our legal representation in the heavenly court.

Paul told the Romans, "I urge you, brothers and sisters, by our Lord Jesus Christ and by the love of the Spirit, to join me in my struggle by praying to God for me."[27] Did you catch that? Paul was asking them to join him in his struggle by praying to God for him. Had you ever pictured yourself when you've prayed as joining with someone in their struggle before the Heavenly Judge? You need to because that is what you are doing when you pray for someone.

This illustration taken from our court system can help you see what has, is now, and will be taking place in the court of heaven before God our Father, who is the Judge of all the earth. Moreover, I hope you will follow the examples of Jesus and Abraham by praying to the Heavenly Judge on behalf of others.

In the second part of Genesis 18, we see a great example of Abraham interceding for the people of Sodom. We also see God, acting as the "Judge of all the earth," hearing the cry of the victims for justice against Sodom and the cities of the plain, going down to visit Sodom before executing justice against it. The story continues into Genesis 19. Let's continue to the next chapter to learn more about the "Judge of all the earth" who is God our Father.

CHAPTER 9
GENESIS 19: JUDGE, JURY AND EXECUTIONER

If you are not reading the chapters in this book in numerical order, then you may want to read Chapter 4 before reading this chapter as I first brought up Sodom and Gomorrah in that chapter when discussing their involvement with Abraham.

We read in the previous chapter that God is the Judge of all the earth and issues judgments from His courtroom in heaven. There is no appellate court above His court. His court is the final court. Justice is extremely important to God.

Here on earth, our judges don't usually execute their sentences themselves. This is done by the police or others in our justice system. Sometimes, that is also the case with God that others execute or carry out His judgments. For example, God stated that "Whoever sheds the blood of man, by man shall his blood be shed, for God made man in his own image."[1] Paul amplified this by stating that "governing authorities" are intended to be "the servant of God, an avenger who carries out God's wrath on the wrongdoer."[2]

However, God sometimes chooses to be the person who executes or carries out His judgments. We are even instructed to leave vengeance to God as He is the best at executing it: "Dear friends, never avenge yourselves. Leave that to God, for he has said that he will repay those who deserve it. Don't take the law into your own hands."[3]

It's always hard for me to read in the Bible when God punishes someone with death. Consider the punishment of Sodom, Gomorrah, and the other cities of the Jordan River Valley. Because of the tragedy we may see when we view God from the eyes of those He has destroyed on this earth, it's hard to see God as a person who wants a loving relationship with us and wants to bless us. It's much more natural for us to put ourselves in the shoes of those who were destroyed on this earth rather than in the shoes of God who did the destroying. But if we fail to put ourselves in God's shoes to gain His perspective on what happened and why, then we are only hearing one side of the story, and that's not fair to God.

Imagine how you would feel if a newspaper reported you injured someone by spraying mace in their face. What if the newspaper reporter didn't ask you what happened and only reported how you had hurt someone else? If you had been consulted, you would've told the reporter that you had sprayed the mace to defend a friend who was being attacked. Spraying the mace in the face of the attacker stopped the attack. Would you feel the reporter was fair to you by not getting your side of the story? Of course not. In the same way, we must be fair to God and spend some time and effort trying to understand the events in these stories from His viewpoint.

Before God destroyed Sodom and Gomorrah, He said to Abraham, "the outcry against Sodom and Gomorrah is great and their sin is very grave."[4] The root word for "outcry"[5] in Hebrew means a "shriek from anguish or danger." Who was making this "great outcry" to God against Sodom and Gomorrah? Why were they crying out to God? What anguish or danger were they experiencing?

When the two angels told Lot (Abraham's nephew) that they planned to stay in the Sodom town square, did you notice Lot "pressed them strongly" to stay at his house instead? This could have been ancient Middle Eastern hospitality at its finest. However, it could also have been because Lot knew what would happen to them if they stayed the night in the town square based on previous experiences he'd witnessed.

Depending on what translation you're reading, you may have slightly different wording in Genesis 19:5 used to state what the men of Sodom said they wanted to do to Lot's two guests. However, in Lot's response to the men of Sodom in verses 6 through 8, it becomes apparent that Lot understood the men wanted to rape Lot's guests. Given Sodom's apparent location between mountains and the Dead Sea,[6] it appears trade routes went through that area and Sodom would have received many overnight visitors. With the great number of people who would have travelled that trade route through that area and the length of time this could have been happening, it's very likely there could've been many thousands of people who would have been violently sexually assaulted in Sodom and the other cities of the plain. The victims' cries of anguish then (and assuming they survived, throughout the remainder of their lives) for the violence they suffered would be the reason why God destroyed these cities. This would essentially be the same reason God destroyed the world in the time of Noah that we read about in Chapter 2 of this book. God hates wickedness because it hurts people, and He will eventually take matters into His own hands to stop it.

Often when I have read this chapter in Genesis, I've dwelt on the tragedy of the death of the people of Sodom or the death of Lot's wife and have missed the mercy of God that is also demonstrated in this story. Let's spend a few minutes here to take a closer look at this story. I believe there are some insights into God's beautiful personality here that are often overlooked.

First, it may appear Sodom and Gomorrah were destroyed suddenly without any chance to repent prior to this. But, I don't believe that to be true now. God had given them the witness and testimony of Lot and Abraham, even using Abraham to rescue them, to turn them from the ways that would lead to their destruction.

Lot came to reside in the area. Living a righteous life in front of them would have been a testimony to all who wanted to seek the Lord. The Bible refers to Lot as a "righteous man" in 2 Peter 2:8; and, it was apparent by the story that he was. He treated the two angels visiting Sodom with great hospitality like Abraham had earlier. The men of Sodom reacted to Lot's refusal to turn over the men like many people do in today's world when encountered with righteousness by stating something like, "Don't you judge us!"[7] In the answer back to Lot, they also referred to him as an outsider and not one of their own. If he had converted to their ways, they most likely would not have referred to him that way. Finally, note that in this story Lot's daughters were still virgins (although they were engaged to be married), and that was probably a unique occurrence in this evil city.

In addition to Lot's witness to the people of the valley, we learn from Genesis 14 that God allowed the people of the cities of the plain to be captured and taken away by other kings many miles to the north of where they lived. The people were later rescued by none other than Abraham. No doubt in that encounter with Abraham, and in the long journey back from near Damascus all the way to south of the Dead Sea area, the people of the cities of the plain must have become acquainted with Abraham, noticing he lived a completely different life from them. Furthermore, in Genesis 14:21–24, Abraham tells the king of Sodom that he has promised the Lord he would not take anything of Sodom's so that they couldn't say they were the source of Abraham's wealth. Looking further into Abraham's statement to the King of Sodom, Abraham describes the Lord as "God Most High, Possessor of heaven and earth." You could read into this that Abraham was trying to get the people of Sodom whom he had rescued to acknowledge the Lord as God: they should submit to the Lord and change their ways. In addition, Abraham's statement that he didn't want the people of Sodom thinking they had made him rich was because it was obvious to everyone: Abraham's wealth was well known. He wanted them to know God had made him rich, again testifying to the goodness of God. So, I believe God allowed the people of Sodom and the other cities of the plain to be captured and then rescued by a righteous man as a way to see what they were doing was wrong and encourage them to change their ways.

The second insight is that God showed He would change His plans and didn't destroy everything He originally intended to destroy. Did you notice how one of the angels told Lot, "Flee for your lives! Don't look back, and don't stop anywhere in the plain! Flee to the mountains or you will be swept away!"[8] We need to quickly discuss the geography of the area to fully understand this. In Genesis 14:2, the five kings of the area and the cities they ruled are listed: Sodom, Gomorrah, Admah, Zeboyim, and Bela. These are referred to in Genesis 13:12 as the "cities of the plain." The angel's statement "don't stop anywhere in the plain," shows God planned to destroy all the cities of the plain, not just Sodom. Lot was being told to leave the plain entirely and go to the mountains.

But in Genesis 19:18–20, Lot tells the angels he can't flee to the mountains. He says he won't be able to make it in time, the disaster will overtake him, and he will die. Lot asks that instead of the mountains, he be allowed to flee to a nearby town that is very small. The angel grants this request and states he won't overthrow the town because of Lot being there. In reading Genesis 19:21–29 and in Genesis 14:2, we can conclude that the very small town was Bela, one of the five cities of the plain mentioned in Genesis 14:2, and its name was changed to Zoar, which means "small"[9] in Hebrew. With this request, Lot has escaped the disaster of God's wrath against the cities of the plain. But not just Lot and his two daughters. And not just the buildings that made up the town of Zoar. I believe the people who lived in the city of Zoar were also saved, even though just earlier that night they had been doomed for destruction like their neighbors. God allowed some wickedness to remain in place so He could avoid also destroying the righteous person Lot.[10]

It's interesting to me that shortly after the destruction of all of the plain but the city of Zoar (formerly known as Bela), Lot chooses to leave Zoar anyway and go to the mountains like the angel had first instructed him. The Bible does not explain why Lot did this. Was it because the people of Zoar remained wicked and were threatening to Lot, and he was fearful to stay any longer? Or did Lot, after realizing God destroyed everything in the plain but this tiny town, become fearful that God wanted to finish the job and decided he needed to move on? We are not told why.

What is especially noteworthy after this is that God did not then rain down fire and brimstone on Zoar after Lot left it. The town of Zoar is referred to numerous times throughout the history of Israel. I wonder why God didn't destroy it as soon as Lot left it. Did the people of Zoar change their behavior after hearing Lot's account of the past 24 hours and seeing the destruction of the rest of the plain? Unfortunately, we won't know the answer to that on this side of heaven. However, the thing to note about this is that God honored what the angel said he would do long after Lot left Zoar. God would have been justified in destroying Zoar after Lot left it, but He didn't. To me, God seems to look for any just reason He can use to keep Himself from destroying them rather than looking for any reason to destroy them. We could conclude then that God does not want to destroy people if He can avoid it. Ezekiel 18:32 confirms this conclusion: "For I have no pleasure in the death of anyone, declares the Lord God; so turn and live."

> **God seems to look for any just reason He can use to keep Himself from destroying them rather than looking for any reason to destroy them.**

To summarize this, God gave the cities of the plain at least two witnesses, and maybe more not recorded in the Bible, as well as time to repent before He destroyed them. He also allowed wicked people who were supposed to be destroyed to live in order that He didn't destroy righteous people with them. Once He wouldn't have destroyed righteous people with them, He didn't finish the destruction but kept the word of His angel not to destroy that small town.

Are there wicked people in your life? People who have harmed you, perhaps even violently? Why does God not execute justice now and destroy them now? Perhaps we see why in how He acted in this story of Lot and the city of Sodom.

I believe God wants to give people time to repent (to figuratively "change direction"), to believe what He says about things and submit to His authority. God would rather wait and not execute judgment against the wicked in hopes that they will change. He hopes they will hear about Jesus's offer to exchange their sins for His righteousness, believe God, and then change their ways to mirror His ways. To give wicked people time to repent requires that wicked people are still able to do wicked things and hurt us and others. In 2 Peter 3:9 it states: "The Lord isn't really being slow about his promise, as some people think. No, he is being patient for your sake. He does not want anyone to be destroyed but wants everyone to repent."[11]

Aren't you glad that God did not decide to destroy all wickedness earlier in history? If He had done so, you may never have been born. Or if you had been born, you might have been one of the wicked, not yet having time to change your ways, and God could have destroyed you. It seems that we are all for God destroying the wicked when it's other people, but when it's us who might be destroyed for our own wickedness, then we would appreciate God giving us more time. Two of Jesus's disciples wanted Jesus to bring down fire from heaven to destroy a village that refused to receive Jesus, but Jesus rebuked the disciples and they went to another village instead.[12] Jesus would rather walk miles to another village rather than destroy the village that rejected Him. Since the Bible says Jesus "expresses the very character" of God the Father,[13] we can assume God the Father would do the same thing; at least until He determines they are not going to change or for other reasons only He knows, He can't wait any longer.

Jesus told a story about a barren fig tree. I think He did this to show that neither He nor His Father are in a hurry to destroy wickedness in hopes that people will change their ways, or bear fruit as in this story:

> Then Jesus told this story: "A man planted a fig tree in his garden and came again and again to see if there was any fruit on it, but he was always disappointed. Finally, he said to his gardener, 'I've waited three years, and there hasn't been a single fig! Cut it down. It's just taking up space in the garden.' The gardener answered, 'Sir, give it one more chance. Leave it another year, and I'll give it special attention and plenty of fertilizer. If we get figs next year, fine. If not, then you can cut it down.'"[14]

All of us are wicked in God's eyes until we decide to submit our lives to be under the authority of Jesus. If you have not yet submitted your life to Jesus, you will incur God's wrath and destruction at some point in your future. But you can avoid the wrath of God by deciding to follow Jesus and let Him rule your life. If you wish to make this decision now, see Appendix A.

I will conclude this chapter with one more example of God's mercy from Genesis 19:16. Lot hesitated to leave Sodom. We are not told any reason why Lot hesitated, but I can imagine several reasons on my own. One possible reason could be that Lot was wealthy when he arrived in the area and was planning how he could take all his possessions with him. This may or may not be the reason, but it is something the Lord has challenged me about recently. Prosperity, blessings and wealth God has given us to bless us can quickly become a liability and tie us down if we are not willing to quickly leave them to follow Christ. We can all be critical of the behavior of Jesus's 12 disciples while they followed Christ, yet they didn't have a problem leaving everything to follow Jesus. It is said of them, "And when they had brought their boats to land, they left everything and followed Him."[15] Could that be said of me? Could it be said of you? Have we left everything to follow Jesus? In this story with Lot, God showed great mercy to Lot and his family by overcoming Lot's hesitancy to leave everything by having the angels grasp Lot's and his family's hands and physically lead them out of the city.

See what cool things we just learned about the judgment, mercy and love of God! Let's keep going as there is much more to understand about Him in our quest to know Him!

CHAPTER 10
GENESIS 20: HE TAKES IT PERSONALLY

We first learned in Genesis 12 that Abraham and Sarah[1] had a practice of telling everyone they met in foreign places that Sarah was his sister. Sarah was very beautiful, and Abraham was afraid if people knew Abraham was Sarah's husband, they would kill him in order to have her. Technically, they were brother and sister since they had the same father, but they had different mothers. Anyway, Abraham does that again in Genesis 20, when he arrives in the land of the Philistines near the city of Gerar. Then, Abimilek, the king of Gerar, "sent for Sarah and took her."[2]

Again, God defends Abraham and comes to Abimilek in a dream. Let's read the interaction between God and Abimilek from the dream from Genesis 20:3–7:

> But God came to Abimelech in a dream by night and said to him, "Behold, you are a dead man because of the woman whom you have taken, for she is a man's wife." Now Abimelech had not approached her. So he said, "Lord, will you kill an innocent people? Did he not himself say to me, 'She is my sister'? And she herself said, 'He

is my brother.' In the integrity of my heart and the innocence of my hands I have done this." Then God said to him in the dream, "Yes, I know that you have done this in the integrity of your heart, and it was I who kept you from sinning against me. Therefore, I did not let you touch her. Now then, return the man's wife, for he is a prophet, so that he will pray for you, and you shall live. But if you do not return her, know that you shall surely die, you and all who are yours."

Notice how God tells Abimelek, "it was I who kept you from sinning against *me*." Did you catch that? God said "me," not "Abraham." That's interesting. Why did God say, "sinning against me" rather than "sinning against Abraham?" As usual, God doesn't explain Himself and we are left to try to put the puzzle pieces together to figure it out. I'll suggest a few possible reasons why.

The first is because God considers all sin as sins against Himself personally. Rather than viewing sin as an offense made against a human being with no impact on Him, God views all sin as an offense performed against Him. Do you consider that strange? I did at one time, but don't any longer. The Apostle Paul wrote in the book of Romans, "For since the creation of the world, God's invisible qualities—his eternal power and divine nature—have been clearly seen, being understood from what has been made, so that people are without excuse."[3] In other words, God made creation in a way that reflects Him, His power and His personality. He worked long and hard to reveal Himself to us in what He has created. So, if that creation suddenly starts acting badly, it distorts the picture He has created of Himself. He interprets that as reflecting poorly on Him. He feels dishonored by the way His creation has started acting.

Here's an illustration to explain the point I am trying to make: Say you are a master chef and invite friends to your house for a backyard dinner where you will make some gourmet pizzas for them. You work hard to make these on the grill and look forward to the thought of your friends eating them and seeing their eyes widen in delight as the tremendous flavor hits their taste buds. That hard work will be well worth it, as it will bring enjoyment to those you care about and allow you to use your talent and expertise to bless them. Your friends know you are a master chef and very much look forward to enjoying the results of your labor. However, one of your guests gets jealous and talks everyone into a game where they throw your pizzas like frisbees! Before long, they have landed in the grass, one or two even landing in some water, and they're no longer edible. The pizzas are no longer the delicious meal intended to display your passion for good food but have instead become the source of laughter and joke-making. At that point, how would you feel about what had just happened? If you are anything like me, you would feel angry, very offended, disrespected and mocked because of something you worked so hard to create: something you were so proud of was made into a joke. You offered your friends your time, talent and food to bless them and instead what you created was misused in a way that didn't reflect you at all.

I think that must be how God feels when we treat any part of His creation (including other human beings made in His image) in a way He did not intend. When God first made all of creation, including humans, He judged all of it and concluded it was not only good, it was "very good."[4] Satan, the jealous person in the pizza analogy I just mentioned, continually tries to get us to misuse and mistreat the rest of God's creation. Therefore, this is why I believe that when we do something that hurts someone else, even though we feel our sin was against that other human being, from God's point of view, it is a sin against Him.

King David, a descendant of Abraham and one of the main characters later in the Old Testament, understood this. After he had sinned terribly, it finally hit him how wrong he was to do what he did. He says to God, "*Against you*, you only, have I sinned and done what is evil in your sight; so you are right in your verdict and justified when you judge."[5] He realized that regardless of whether our sins affect other people or not, they affect God.

I think Joseph, a great-grandson of Abraham, understood this. In Genesis 39:8–9 (NIV, italics added for emphasis), he tells his master's wife who is trying to seduce him: "With me in charge," he told her, "my master does not concern himself with anything in the house; everything he owns he has entrusted to my care. No one is greater in this house than I am. My master has withheld nothing from me except you, because you are his wife. How then could I do such a wicked thing *and sin against God?*"

Did you notice how after telling his master's wife how his master trusted him, it would sound natural for Joseph to say, "How then could I do such a wicked thing and sin against [my master]." However, that is not what Joseph says. He says, "How then could I do such a wicked thing and sin against God?"

There's a second possible reason why God may have said "sinning against me" rather than "sinning against Abraham." I believe God hurts when we hurt. He views our hurt as His hurt, our pain as His pain. Would it surprise you to know our Creator who made us, who intimately knows how we feel and think, and who loves us very much, would hurt when we hurt? If it does surprise you, I urge you to visit the waiting room of a pediatric hospital unit. Notice how the parents of children who are suffering are in emotional turmoil. While they may look OK on the outside, they are hurting on the inside for their children. If you could see inside their hearts, their pain would be as plain as day. It's the same with our loving Father God. When one human being violates another human being and creates pain and loss, God grieves.

The third reason God may have said, "sinning against me" is that God and Abraham were in a covenant together. If you are in a covenant with someone, you are in a type of treaty with them. If you and I are in covenant with each other and someone attacks you, I should view it as if they had attacked me. I would be expected to come to your defense! And if I were attacked, you would be expected to come to my defense.

These are the three reasons I suggest why God responded to Abimilek as He did. I don't think these reasons are mutually exclusive, so I believe all three of the above may be reasons why God responded like He did. How about you?

I find it interesting that in the same way God told Abimilek that Abimilek was sinning against Him by taking Abraham's wife Sarah, Jesus says something very similar to Saul when Jesus confronted Saul on the road to Damascus: "He [Saul] fell to the ground and heard a voice say to him, 'Saul, Saul, why do you persecute me?' 'Who are you, Lord?' Saul asked. 'I am Jesus, *whom you are persecuting*,' he replied."[6]

Jesus had already ascended into heaven when Saul was persecuting the early church, so Saul had not actually laid a hand on Jesus himself. Yet, Jesus viewed Saul's actions of persecution of others as persecution of Himself.

I find it comforting to realize that when I hurt, God hurts. He is not ambivalent when it comes to you. He cares. He is not some distant god who has to be convinced to care about you. And in those times of suffering and hurt, His heart hurts and aches too.

CHAPTER 11
GENESIS 21: IT COMES TO PASS

Genesis 21 opens with God's promise to Abraham finally coming to pass. One-hundred-year-old Abraham and 90-year-old Sarah have their promised son from God. Abraham names their son "Isaac" as God commanded[1] which means "laughter."[2] God has done what He said He would do.

Sarah is probably the most ecstatic of anyone. She says, "God has brought me laughter, and everyone who hears about this will laugh with me."[3] Her sense of relief from finally having the son God had promised must have been enormous, as she undoubtedly had felt tremendous pressure to give Abraham a son. I'm sure she had been told by Abraham what God had promised him after every encounter he had with God. I can just picture poor Sarah listening to Abraham share with great enthusiasm what God had just told him. Then Sarah might have felt a tremendous disconnect when reality hits her again that she has not ever had a child and is quite old already.

Remember in Genesis 16 when Sarai (Sarah's name in that chapter) came up with the idea of giving Hagar, her servant, to Abraham for him to sleep with her and to have a child by her? This idea was probably born out of the great mental anguish she had undoubtedly suffered trying on her own to somehow bring God's promise to pass and give a son to Abraham. It would seem all emotional distress and disappointment was now gone, as God had done the impossible and given her a son through Abraham.

Life was great for Sarah after the birth of Isaac. Or was it? Now whenever she looked at Ishmael and Hagar, instead of seeing the result of her selfless act of giving her husband a son through her servant, she saw a rival for her and her son. Whenever Abraham came out of the fields for the day, he was greeted not just by Sarah and her now two-year-old son Isaac, but also by Ishmael whom Abraham also undoubtedly loved. After all, Ishmael was also Abraham's son.

Ishmael was now about 16 years old and surely interacted on a different level than did Isaac. Ishmael would have been trained by Abraham in the ways of the Lord, learned Abraham's genealogy all the way back to Adam and quoted that and other things Abraham had taught him to know to pass on down to his children. Ishmael would have assisted Abraham with preparing offerings and sacrifices, things Isaac could not physically do yet. So, then, at the great feast Abraham held to celebrate Isaac's weaning, it is foreseeable that an obnoxious 16-year old may make fun of his two-year-old half-brother and in doing so, incur the wrath of Sarah against him like a mother bear protecting her cubs from an enemy.

Abraham was horribly distressed[4] as Sarah now demands "get rid of that slave woman and her son, for that woman's son will never share in the inheritance with my son Isaac."[5] Wait a minute! Ishmael was also his [Abraham's] son! Until about three years ago, Abraham had thought for more than a decade that Ishmael was the descendant God had promised him. How could he now disinherit Ishmael? What's more, how could he send his beloved son Ishmael away? The years had bonded the hearts of Abraham and Ishmael together. Oh, how great the emotional loss Abraham would feel from sending Ishmael away. I can only imagine the thoughts going on between Abraham and Sarah as they undoubtedly argued back and forth about this.

It is at this point that God gets involved in the scene and tells Abraham, "Do not be so distressed about the boy and your slave woman. Listen to whatever Sarah tells you, because it is through Isaac that your offspring will be reckoned. I will make the son of the slave into a nation also, because he is your offspring."[6] God's statement to Abraham helps Abraham come to terms with what Sarah is demanding. I would suggest that it was only by God's intervention in speaking to Abraham about the matter and God's promise to make him into a nation that this matter is resolved.

Note that Abraham didn't take a month or so to say goodbye to Ishmael. Once God spoke to Abraham what to do, Abraham did it immediately, regardless of the pain it might cause him. "Early the next morning,"[7] Abraham acts. This is an attribute of Abraham's that we have seen several times now. Once God speaks to him, he immediately acts in obedience to God.

I have struggled with why God would allow Sarah to get her way in this matter. It was Sarah's idea in the first place to give Hagar to Abraham to produce a child. Why not make her live with the consequences of what she did with Abraham many years ago? To use a phrase we use in the Midwest, why didn't God make them all "get along" instead of having Ishmael and Hagar leave? Especially in the way that Abraham sent them away, with just enough food and water that Hagar herself could carry?[8] That wouldn't last them very long.

Abraham must have believed God would intervene to make sure they survived. And not just survived but thrive so that Ishmael would also be made into a nation of his own. That is exactly what God did. God kept His word. He called to Hagar from heaven and encouraged her just when she needed it. Hagar and Ishmael had wandered for days, run out of water and given up all hope of life. He showed her water and probably did even more than what is mentioned in the Bible. This further assistance is probably summarized by the simple statement, "God was with the boy as he grew up." As the Bible implies throughout all its pages and in even the worst of circumstances, when God is with you, you will be all right. Maybe not in the ways other people in this world would associate with success, or in the ways you would prefer, but you will be all right because God is with you.

But Ishmael and Hagar's survival and success doesn't fully help me understand why God would allow Sarah to get her way and have Ishmael and Hagar sent away. God's taking care of them is great, but it doesn't make up for the loss that Abraham must have felt for his son, Ishmael.

This isn't the first time that I've had a question like this as to why God did things or allowed things to happen the way He did in the Bible. I've had lots of them over my lifetime. New ones pop up all the time. And eventually so do the answers for most of them. Sometimes the answers pop up when I'm reading other parts of the Bible, and sometimes I have to wait many years for the answer. Sometimes I get an answer only to get an even better answer later. The point is to keep looking and not give up and most of all not stop believing. As Jesus said, "Ask and it will be given to you; seek and you will find; knock and the door will be opened to you."[9] He didn't say that you would get what you ask immediately. It's so cool when your asking, seeking and knocking are finally rewarded with an answer.

In this particular case, I believe the reason why God allowed Ishmael to be sent away was because He wanted Abraham's heart to be completely invested in Isaac's life. God wanted Abraham to have no other child to fall back on in which he might think God's promises could be fulfilled, other than Isaac. He wanted Abraham to think of Isaac as his *only* son. This is even how God refers to Isaac in Genesis 22, as Abraham's only son. The child to be born from 90-year-old Sarah was the fulfillment of the promises. It was very important to God for Abraham to think his only child was Isaac. Why? We will learn the answer in our next chapter covering Genesis 22.

In the meantime, I want to share a "and they lived happily ever after" moment involving Ishmael with you. If you skip forward to

Genesis 23 and 25, you'll read that Sarah lived to the age of 127 before she passed away. She died having no other children but Isaac. Her death was many years before Abraham's death at the age of 175, so Abraham has another wife after Sarah named Keturah and they have many other children together. Like Ishmael, Abraham sends them away from his son Isaac to the land of the east, but this time, he gives them gifts before sending them away. However, when Abraham dies, Isaac and Ishmael are both there to bury him. Further, verses 12 to 18 of Genesis 25 tell us the names of Ishmael's twelve sons and the age of Ishmael when he died. Finally, the story of how God helped Hagar and Ishmael survive in the desert in Genesis 21:15–21 would probably not be known to us unless Ishmael had shared this story with Abraham, Isaac, or both of them.

This leads me to believe that while they lived separately, Abraham and Isaac had, at some point before Abraham's death, reestablished communications and relationship with Ishmael. God kept His word to Abraham and blessed Ishmael by being with him, even though he was apart from Abraham.

I think the events in Genesis 22 (the next chapter) take place before Abraham and Isaac reconnect with Ishmael. Why do I think the relationship with Ishmael was re-established after the events of Genesis 22 and not before? Well, I don't want to spoil it for you. Read on to find out what God was going to share with His friend Abraham in such an unusual and powerful way. Information that Abraham and his descendants did not fully understand until about 1,900 years later, after the resurrection of Jesus Christ from the dead.

And remember, when God says He will do something, He does it.

CHAPTER 12
GENESIS 22: HOW GOD FELT

Empathy can be defined as "the capacity to understand or feel what another person is experiencing from within their frame of reference, that is, the capacity to place oneself in another's position."[1] It is an important quality to possess. Without it, we can't comprehend the level of pain someone else may be feeling or understand their actions. Their actions won't make sense to us since we don't feel the same pain they are feeling. While we can have some empathy for other people without going through the same circumstances they are, there is no better way to understand how someone else is feeling than to somehow experience some of what they are going through. There is an old saying that goes something like, "Don't criticize someone unless you first walk a mile in their shoes."

For example, I had witnessed other people who had a child die when I was younger and had no children of my own. I thought I understood how they hurt and grieved. However, it was not until I had children of my own that I could start to grasp how deep and painful that hurt and grief could be. Fortunately, I have not had the experience of losing a child, so I still don't fully know what it would be like, but I can better understand it now as a parent compared to when I was a childless young adult.

I've started out this chapter discussing empathy because it is huge in understanding what takes place in the Bible, and probably no more important than here in Genesis 22.

Genesis 22 starts out with a shocking request that God makes of His friend Abraham: "After these things God tested Abraham and said to him, 'Abraham!' And he said, 'Here I am.' He said, 'Take your son, your only son Isaac, whom you love, and go to the land of Moriah, and offer him there as a burnt offering on one of the mountains of which I shall tell you.'"[2]

How could God request something like that of anyone, let alone Abraham?! He knew Isaac was Abraham's only son, didn't He? He knew how long Abraham had waited to see his son Isaac become a reality, didn't He? Of course, He did! He states, "take your son" and then adds insult to injury and adds, "your only son Isaac." How could God do that? God even adds the words, "whom you love" as if putting one final stake in Abraham's heart was needed because the earlier words didn't do enough to pierce Abraham's heart.

To my surprise, Abraham doesn't question God at all. The next verse says that "Abraham rose early in the morning, saddled his donkey, and took two of his young men with him, and his son Isaac. And he cut the wood for the burnt offering and arose and went to the place of which God had told him." If Abraham is like me at all, one of the reasons he rose early was because he didn't get an ounce of sleep after that conversation with God. He had to have had a thousand questions with no acceptable answers going through his mind.

- Why would God ask him to sacrifice Isaac? Abraham loved Isaac! He was his son!
- Why did God make all these promises about Abraham becoming a nation through Isaac if he now had to sacrifice Isaac? God had recently clarified to him that it was through Isaac that his descendants would be as numerous

as the sand by the seashore. He had him send his other son Ishmael away after God told him that Isaac was to be his only heir through which the promise would be fulfilled. Ishmael was now gone and out of the picture. God giving Abraham another son wouldn't help because the promises were tied to Isaac. Isaac was it. Only Isaac.

- What would he tell Isaac? Could he somehow keep this from Isaac, or would Isaac find out?
- What would he tell Sarah when he comes back without Isaac? Isaac was her only son too.
- Does God realize that by sacrificing Isaac, Abraham will be childless again? He has no other son to take Isaac's place! He had waited so long to have God's unbelievable promise fulfilled to him, and it came true! Now this!
- Had he or Isaac done something wrong? God seemed to be pleased with him, but maybe God was angry with him and had not told him yet? Had Isaac done something wrong?
- If someone had to die as a sacrifice, why couldn't he [Abraham] die instead of Isaac?
- If Isaac had to die, then why did Abraham need to be the one to kill Isaac? Couldn't God do this Himself if this had to be done?

I am sure Abraham struggled with all of these questions all night as he would have tossed and turned, hoping that if he turned on his other side that the circumstance God just put him in would somehow change back to the wonderful way things had been with his son of promise, Isaac, in his life. However, with more and more thought, he must have come to the realization that there was no way out of this box. All of God's promises to him were to have their fulfillment in Isaac's life, and yet God now not asked, but commanded him to offer Isaac to God as a sacrifice. This required Abraham to put a knife into Isaac and end his precious son's life! And then not even be able to hold him one last time before burying him, but instead to burn him on an altar of sacrifice!

Yet somehow, Abraham chose to believe God to the extent that he would obey God even with sacrificing his and Sarah's one and only son. He had an absolute faith that God would somehow keep His promise, by what means Abraham didn't yet know. Abraham didn't have to know as he trusted God absolutely, believing God would raise Isaac up from the dead somehow in order to keep His promise.

So, Abraham rises early in the morning, with a firmness in his steps and actions. He can't allow himself to question the insanity of what he was about to do, because if he did, he may instead waiver and not do what God had told him to do.

If only the place where God wanted him to do this was close by, but it wasn't. They had to set out on a journey not knowing where he was going, but God would show him. It was not until the third day of their journey that Abraham's eyes saw the place where God told him that He wanted this to happen:

> On the third day Abraham lifted up his eyes and saw the place from afar. Then Abraham said to his young men, "Stay here with the donkey; I and the boy will go over there and worship and come again to you." ⁶And Abraham took the wood of the burnt offering and laid it on Isaac his son. And he took in his hand the fire and the knife. So they went both of them together (Genesis 22:4–6).

Can you imagine the conversations they had those three days on the way there? It must have been hard for Abraham to keep his emotions restrained all that time. Three long days to comprehend the loss of Isaac. The awkwardness of all that time must have weighed on not only Abraham, but also Isaac, as he notices that his father is not as talkative as he was usually. Normally, they would talk about what they are seeing as they walk, as any father and son would. Not this time. Isaac can sense something is different.

Finally, once the servants have been left behind, Isaac can ask his father something that has been bothering him ever since they left home. Now he can ask the question without embarrassing his father in front of his servants. Isaac finally blurts out, "My father! Behold, the fire and the wood, but where is the lamb for a burnt offering?" Abraham replies, "God will provide for Himself the lamb for a burnt offering, my son." With that simple answer, Isaac continues on and carries the wood for the offering, not realizing he is carrying the wood on which he is going to be sacrificed.

Abraham and Isaac finally reach the place and stop their walking and begin the work of preparing to offer the sacrifice. Both Isaac and Abraham begin gathering large stones to build the altar. With Abraham's age now well over 100 years old, I picture Abraham picking out the stones and Isaac doing the heavy lifting of building the altar. How ironic and sad it is that Isaac is building his own altar! Not only did he carry the wood, now he is building the altar too! Abraham finally arranges on the altar the wood Isaac had carried.

Finally, all the preparations had been made. Isaac probably expected to wait now for God to provide the lamb, as his father had said. But instead of resting and waiting, his father begins to bind him with rope! Abraham would not have been able to bind him in one or two seconds. This would take probably at least a minute to do, and maybe longer if Isaac resisted. Can you imagine the hurt that Abraham must have felt looking into his son's beautiful eyes, seeing the fear that Isaac must have felt come through them as Abraham began to bind Isaac and put him on the altar, as Isaac now realized HE was the sacrifice his father said God was going to provide?

Oh, how hard that must have been for Abraham to block out his emotions in order to continue to bind Isaac! But Abraham had chosen to believe and trust God. What else could he do if he were to continue to believe and trust God? Nothing else. The only thing Abraham could do now if he wanted to remain obedient to God is described in a simple sentence: "Then Abraham reached out his hand and took the knife to slaughter his son."[3]

Abraham had offered many offerings to the Lord before when he had to kill an unblemished animal he had raised from its birth and have it all consumed before him on an altar to the Lord. While that may have hurt some to be so ruthless with an animal in taking its life, he had done it so many times and understood this was just an animal that would eventually be killed for its meat and hide. But this was his son, his one and only son, by which God had promised many great things for him, and none of them could come to pass except through Isaac! This was what he was now sacrificing to the God that he obeyed.

Thankfully, God does intervene in this story! At the very last second, God stops Abraham from sacrificing Isaac. God says to him, "Do not lay your hand on the boy or do anything to him, for now I know that you fear God, seeing you have not withheld your son, your only son, from me."[4] Abraham is found faithful in God's eyes. God knows that Abraham would not hold back his son, his only son from God. God then provided the sacrifice by showing Abraham a ram caught by its horns in a thicket which Abraham took and offered as the sacrifice instead of Isaac.

• • •

I started this chapter explaining empathy in order to help you understand the emotional pain and internal conflict that Abraham must have gone through during those three long days in his life. Yes, he believed God that somehow the promise of all of Abraham's descendants coming through Isaac would be fulfilled. But how? Abraham didn't have this story in front of him so that he could quickly read the ending and see that everything works out fine. He was living this story and did not know how this would turn out! Those three days must have been agonizing for Abraham. Abraham was a human being with affections, emotions, fears and dreams, just like you and me. These were probably the three longest and hardest days of Abraham's life. We can read this story in a matter of a few minutes and not comprehend the enormity of all that took place in those three long days. Hopefully, you've been able to empathize and identify with Abraham, seeing things from his point of view.

Because of Abraham's faithfulness, he is mentioned in what some call the "Bible's faith hall of fame," which is Hebrews 11. It says the following about Abraham's actions:

> By faith Abraham, when God tested him, offered Isaac as a sacrifice. He who had embraced the promises was about to sacrifice his one and only son, even though God had said to him, "It is through Isaac that your offspring will be reckoned." Abraham reasoned that God could even raise the dead, and so in a manner of speaking he did receive Isaac back from death (Hebrews 11:17–19, NIV).

However, this book you are reading isn't about Abraham. This book is about God the Father. So, what was God the Father's role in this story? Is He somewhat of a twisted villain, after being the one to cause such emotional pain and distress for Abraham, but makes up for it by providing the ram for the sacrifice? If you are like me, you are probably asking why God put Abraham through all of that only to provide the sacrificial ram at the last minute?

God does speak after all of this happens:

> And the angel of the Lord called to Abraham a second time from heaven and said, "By myself I have sworn, declares the Lord, because you have done this and have not withheld your son, your only son, I will surely bless you, and I will surely multiply your offspring as the stars of heaven and as the sand that is on the seashore. And your offspring shall possess the gate of his enemies, and in your offspring shall all the nations of the earth be blessed, because you have obeyed my voice" (Genesis 22:15–18).

If you look at what God told Abraham, it is pretty much the same as what God had told Abraham previously several times. It wasn't that by Abraham obeying God this time, it set him on a new level with God that He had not attained before. So, what purpose was accomplished with God telling Abraham to do this and Abraham doing what God said to do? Did God need to see if Abraham was the real thing and really believed God? I don't think so, because in an earlier chapter of Genesis God says, "Shall I hide from Abraham what I am about to do, seeing that Abraham shall surely become a great and mighty nation, and all the nations of the earth shall be blessed in him?"[5] So, why would God put Abraham through this emotional trial?

To me, the answer is that God was wanting us to understand what He (God the Father) was going to go through when He sent His Son, His only Son, Jesus to die on a cross for the sins of you, me, and the whole world. You see, God the Father went through the same things that Abraham went through when He sent Jesus to die on the cross for us. Just like Abraham was offering up his only son, so was God the Father. Except God the Father did not have anyone to say, "Stop!" and to provide a substitute. It was His Son, Jesus, the Son of God, who actually became the ultimate sacrifice. And if we are able to empathize with Abraham and understand what he must have gone through emotionally to offer up his one and only son, then perhaps we can now identify with God the Father and what He must have gone through in offering up His one and only Son for all of us. So, I believe God had Abraham go through this horrible experience in order for us to understand what God the Father would go through when He offered up Jesus.

Just like Isaac left his home to go with Abraham to be the sacrifice, Jesus had to leave His place in Heaven to come to this earth where His Father had led Him to die for our sins. Like Isaac, Jesus also carried the wood that was to be used in His sacrifice. In Jesus's case, this was a wooden cross that He carried. Since Jesus created the world, He actually also built the stones that created the mount upon which He would be crucified. Instead of building an altar from stones, like Isaac, He actually built the mount. In fact, Mount Moriah where Isaac was offered is part of Jerusalem, so God had Abraham travel for three days and about 50 miles in order to link the sacrifice of Isaac and Jesus geographically.

Jesus was bound like Isaac, but Jesus was not rescued at the last second by someone providing the real sacrifice. Jesus was the real intended sacrifice. God intended for Jesus to die to pay the penalty for all sin.

I also believe that one of the reasons Ishmael was sent away from Abraham before all this happened is that God didn't want Abraham thinking it would be OK to offer Isaac as a sacrifice because Abraham still had another son, Ishmael, through which God could give him descendants. God wanted Abraham to understand that he was offering to God his *only* son through which Abraham would ever have descendants. By Abraham understanding that Isaac was his only son, the parallel of Abraham sacrificing Isaac and God the Father sacrificing His one and only Son Jesus is perfected.

I don't know if we will ever grasp how much pain and hurt was going through God the Father's heart as He heard His only beloved Son say, "My God, My God, why have you forsaken me?" How hard it must have been for God the Father to turn His face away from Jesus and resist saving Him from the death that He did not deserve. Ponder this! Think about it! God the Father must have experienced tremendous hurt in seeing His one and only Son beaten, mocked and then crucified. Somehow, He held Himself back from rescuing Jesus because there was no other way for Him to save us if He did!

Now, like was said by God of Abraham, may we say of God the Father, "Now I know that you [love me], because you have not withheld from me your son, your only son."[6] And now we understand more fully the love of God the Father that Jesus was describing when Jesus said in John 3:16, "For God so loved the world, that he gave his only Son, that whoever believes in him should not perish but have eternal life." The word "so" needs to be emphasized somehow, because He didn't just love the world some, but He "SO" loved the world if He was willing to put Himself and his son Jesus through that for you and me.

With this in mind, it means a lot more when we read in I John 4:19, "We love him [God], because He first loved us."[7]

I hope you will not just simply turn the page to start another chapter but will pause for a minute to think about what physical and emotional pain both God the Father and Jesus the Son went through for you. May the reality of that sink deep into your heart. May the love of God for you that drove God the Father to offer His one and only Son fill your heart and capture it. You were the object of that love. Don't let that love be in vain. Return that love to Him.

CHAPTER 13
GENESIS 25: TURNING THINGS UPSIDE DOWN

Much time goes by after the events of Genesis 22 before we see God act or speak directly regarding anything major from which we can learn something about Him. A period of at least 20 and possibly 50 years goes by. Oh, that doesn't mean that God went off and took a vacation or sabbatical after having His plan to redeem humankind demonstrated by asking Abraham to offer up Isaac. He is very much involved in helping Abraham's servant find Rebekah, the girl who would become Isaac's wife. He is also involved in Abraham's and Isaac's lives, continuing to bless them and be with them. It's just that not a lot of details of His involvement in these events is recorded in the Bible to learn from them. I might pause to say that in the same way, God is active in your life today. You may not record them or even be aware of them yourself. But believe it; He is not only watching but involved.

In Genesis 25, God has a major, albeit brief role. He speaks something short but powerful to Rebekah, who is concerned because of what is going on in her body after she's become pregnant. She inquires of the Lord and He says: "Two nations are in your womb, and two peoples from within you shall be divided; the one shall be stronger than the other, the older shall serve the younger."[1]

What news! Twins! Remember, this was before sonograms. God gives Rebekah some assurance that things are OK by telling her she is carrying twins and they are already struggling with each other inside of her.[2] This was the reason for all the activity within her. But God shared something even more important considering the order of family life at that time. In the case of Rebekah's children, the older child would serve the younger. This was in stark contrast to culture at that time.

This would not be the only time where the younger child in the Bible would get the blessing over the older child. Jacob, the younger of Rebekah's twins, later replicates this when giving his blessing to the sons of Joseph, his son. Jacob (named "Israel" at this point in his life) purposefully places his right hand on the head of Joseph's younger son, Ephraim, and his left hand on the head of Joseph's younger son, Manasseh, when praying a blessing for them. Further, when Joseph tries to correct his father's apparent mistake, perhaps thinking it is because of his dad's poor eyesight that his dad put his right hand on the youngest child, Jacob insists that he knows what he is doing and tells Joseph the younger child shall be greater than the older child.[3]

Another famous instance of the younger child being chosen ahead of older children happened later in the Old Testament when God told the prophet Samuel that the next king of Israel would be one of the sons of Jesse, of the tribe of Judah.[4] Samuel goes to Jesse's town and seeing the oldest son, assumes God wants him to be the next king. Then God says something telling about how He sees people. He tells Samuel, "Don't judge by a man's face or height, for this is not the one. I don't make decisions the way you do! Men judge by outward appearance, but I look at a man's thoughts and intentions."[5] So Samuel continues to examine all of Jesse's sons until he's looked at all seven of Jesse's sons put in front of him. But God tells Samuel that none of these seven are the one God wants. This must have been very confusing for Samuel. Samuel then asks Jesse, "Are these all the sons you have?" and Jesse says, "There is still the youngest. He is tending the sheep."[6] Apparently, Jesse didn't think the youngest was important enough to join the rest of the family in a banquet with Samuel. Now Jesse sends for the youngest at Samuel's request. When Samuel sees David, God says, "Rise and anoint him; this is the one."[7] Here again, the youngest is the preferred one in God's eyes.

Did you catch the *huge* thing God said about Himself to Samuel? Let's take a moment to stop at this, and then we'll resume this chapter. God said to Samuel, "I don't make decisions the way you do! Men judge by outward appearance, but I look at man's thoughts and intentions."[8] This is an important thing to remember about God. He sees our hearts, with its various thoughts and motives. While He knows what our bodies look like, that is not how He views us. He regards us by what He sees in our hearts, something which can't be seen by a mere man. We can dress up our lives with lots of good works and other things hoping to please God, but if our heart is hiding hatred and lust underneath all those good works, while we might appear to be a good person to others, in God's eyes we are not. We are to Him what is in our hearts.

While we can't easily see the hearts of others, we can try to stop seeing people by their outward appearance. We can learn to recognize this about ourselves and start trying to disregard age, beauty, physical attraction, fitness, skin color, racial heritage and other things we see with our eyes and start trying to view people as God might see them, reserving judgment on people until we see evidence of what might be in their hearts. Martin Luther King, Jr. said in his famous "I have a dream" speech, "I have a dream that my four little children will one day live in a nation where they will not be judged by the color of their skin but by the content of their character." I wholeheartedly agree with his statement and hope that all of us could realize how we see people today and start trying to see people as God sees them, seeing the "hidden man of the heart" rather than "fancy hairstyles, expensive jewelry or beautiful clothes."[9]

Now, getting back to the content of this chapter, am I suggesting that this is always the case, God choosing the younger child over the oldest? No. However, I am suggesting that God sometimes upsets the proverbial "apple cart." He does turn things we trust in, besides Him, upside down. In Old Testament times, picking the younger child over the older child was a way to do this. Said another way, He does sometimes like to mess up people's plans, especially when those plans exalt humankind and don't acknowledge Him.[10] He likes to show that He is still in charge, but not for his own ego as I would perhaps do, but because knowing Him is eternal life itself,[11] and apart from Him we are hopeless.[12] So, He upsets the status quo to remind us that we need Him and that we should submit to Him rather than strive against Him.

As you've read this chapter, some of you may be thinking that I'm reaching too far in applying the above points from the Old Testament to come up with this conclusion about God. Well, you could have a point because I am not perfect. So, let's do this. Jesus, the Son of God, is the "exact representation of his [God the Father's] being."[13] Therefore, if there is a personality trait about God the Father, then that personality trait should also show up in the words and ministry of Jesus, God the Son, as recorded in the New Testament as well as in those of Jesus's disciples. Based on the below points, I believe this desire to turn things upside down also shows up in Jesus:

- Jesus is quoted several times in the gospels saying, "But many that are first shall be last; and the last shall be first" (Matthew 19:30, KJV), or something similar to this.[14] In the context of these statements, he is saying that many people in this life work so hard to achieve greatness and trust in their riches, but while they may be great in this world, they will be poor and miserable in the life to come. In the same way, many who appear not to have much money and aren't successful in this world's eyes, will be lauded as heroes in Jesus's kingdom in heaven, because they put God's desires above their own in this world.[15] An upside down in both directions!

- In the book of Revelation, Jesus says to the church of Laodicea, "You say, 'I am rich, with everything I want; I don't need a thing!' And you don't realize that spiritually you are wretched and miserable and poor and blind and naked."[16] How would you like to be called, "wretched," especially by Jesus? I wouldn't. If nothing changes, this church that sees itself doing so well will have an ugly awakening to the truth of how God sees it. Their thoughts of themselves will be turned upside down.

- Paul said in the book of Corinthians, "Notice among yourselves, dear brothers, that few of you who follow Christ have big names or power or wealth. Instead, God has deliberately chosen to use ideas the world considers foolish and of little worth in order to shame those people considered by the world as wise and great. He has chosen a plan despised by the world, counted as nothing at all, and used it to *bring down to nothing* those the world considers great, so that no one anywhere can ever brag in the presence of God" (1 Corinthians 1:26–29, TLB, italics added for emphasis). Another thing turned upside down.

- James wrote in his letter to the church, "And he gives grace generously. As the scriptures say, 'God opposes the proud but gives grace to the humble.' So humble yourselves before God. Resist the devil, and he will flee from you. Come close to God, and God will come close to you. Wash your hands, you sinners; purify your hearts, for your loyalty is divided between God and the world. Let there be tears for what you have done. Let there be sorrow and deep grief. Let there be sadness instead of laughter, and gloom instead of joy. *Humble yourselves before the Lord, and he will lift you up in honor*" (James 4:6–10, NLT, italics added for emphasis). James is warning them to be sorry for their sins so God can turn that sorrow upside down into joy. Otherwise, God will turn their joy upside down into sorrow in response to their sin.

- I find it interesting that even nonbelievers saw what God was doing through the early church when they reported, "These men who have *turned the world upside down* have come here also" (Acts 17:6, italics added for emphasis). They thought it was men turning the world upside down because they didn't know the Mighty God who was working through these men chooses to turn things we trust in other than Him upside down!

One of the most challenging to us of God's "upside downs" came to us through a challenge from Jesus. The world was seeing the healings, miracles and other wonders Jesus was performing and coming after Him to follow Him as a political star. It was cool to follow Jesus at that point. Then Jesus turns things upside down, so people would think twice about following Him. Here is what Luke says about this "upside down."

> A large crowd was following Jesus. He turned around and said to them, 'If you want to be my disciple, you must, by comparison, hate everyone else—your father and mother, wife and children, brothers and sisters—yes, even your own life. Otherwise, you cannot be my disciple. And if you do not carry your own cross and follow me, you cannot be my disciple (Luke 14:25–27, NLT).

In Jesus's time, a cross was not something pretty put on top of buildings or worn around their necks. A cross was used to execute someone with an excruciating death. In today's terms, Jesus would be telling us to take up our electric chair and follow Him. Jesus was essentially telling them they had to turn their life upside down by loving Him more than anyone else in this world, including themselves, in order to follow Him. That's quite the demand Jesus is making, isn't it? When you consider how He turned His own existence upside down for our benefit, He has not asked us to do anything beyond what He has already done for us.

> Though he was God, he did not think of equality with God as something to cling to. Instead, he gave up his divine privileges; he took the humble position of a slave and was born as a human being. When he appeared in human form, he humbled himself in obedience to God and died a criminal's death on a cross. Therefore, God elevated him to the place of highest honor and gave him the name above all other names, that at the name of Jesus every knee should bow, in heaven and on earth and under the earth, and every tongue declare that Jesus Christ is Lord, to the glory of God the Father (Philippians 2:6–11, NLT).

Jesus turned His own life upside down by leaving heaven and giving up all He deserved so He could be obedient to God the Father. God the Father, in turn, honored Him for His obedience by turning His death upside down by raising Him from the dead and exalting Him above all. Wow, the greatest "upside down" of all time!

So, let's conclude that God is a master at doing "upside downs," making low those who have exalted themselves and exalting those who have made themselves low in obeying Him.

Has God done an upside down in your life yet? If not, He will. Are you trusting yourself to make your life the best or are you sacrificing this life to God and trusting Him to make your life great in His own way?

If you're currently wealthy, powerful and seem to have everything going for you, be prepared to be made poor and lowly. Better yet, follow Jesus and turn your wealth and life over to Him. God can give you much more than what you have surrendered to Him.

If you're currently following Jesus and loving Him above all else in your life, look for God to do an upside down for you, blessing you in this life and the life to come!

CHAPTER 14
GENESIS 26–36: HOLDING ON

The next 11 chapters of Genesis are filled primarily with the actions of Isaac and his sons, Esau and Jacob, but God is active behind the scenes bringing to pass the things that will cause all nations of the earth to be blessed through Abraham's offspring:

- God speaks to Isaac, making the same promises to him that were made to Abraham: being with him, blessing him, giving him innumerable descendants, giving him the land where he was and blessing all nations of the earth through his offspring.[1]
- Jacob becomes the son of Isaac who inherits these promises of God,[2] even though he is not the oldest son, contrary to the customs of that age. God still blesses Esau,[3] but Jacob is the one through whom God's covenant promises to Abraham will be fulfilled.
- Jacob makes a vow of conditional allegiance to God after God appears to him in a dream.[4] At this point, his

viewpoint of God is almost like that of a genie. Jacob uses a "IF-THEN" statement, almost like he was using computer code to describe his relationship with God. His allegiance is conditioned upon:

- o IF God is with him and watches over [takes care of] him
- o IF God gives him food and clothing
- o IF Jacob returns to his father's house safely
- o THEN, the Lord will be my God
- o THEN, this stone I have set up will be God's house
- o THEN, I will give 10% to God of all that He gives me[5]

- God, in fact, blesses Jacob, giving him wives, children and much wealth. He then tells Jacob to return home,[6] which Jacob is happy to do seeing how his relationship with Laban, his father-in-law, has become hostile.[7]
- Like what God did for his grandfather Abraham,[8] God speaks in a dream to defend Jacob from his father-in-law, Laban.[9]
- Jacob returns to the land, and God sends angels to meet him.[10]
- Jacob prepares to meet his brother Esau and is fearful Esau will want to kill him. Jacob calls out to God for help with a new attitude toward God, saying he is unworthy of all the kindness and faithfulness God has shown him since he left this land and made his vow to God some 20 years ago.[11]
- On the night before Jacob is to meet Esau, Jacob has sent everyone else on ahead and is alone. He wrestles with someone who he first thought was a man but then discovers was God. God blesses him there and gives him the name "Israel."[12]

- Jacob and Esau meet. Esau shows kindness toward Jacob. Apparently still wary of Esau, Jacob says he will follow Esau back to Seir, but instead goes to Shechem.[13]
- Jacob's daughter Dinah is raped there. Her brothers, in retaliation, trick all the men of that city. Two of them kill all the men of Shechem, and all the brothers take everything and everyone remaining as plunder. Jacob is angry at Simeon and Levi for this and worries that all of them will be attacked as a result.[14]
- God tells Jacob to move to Bethel and Jacob settles there.[15]
- At Bethel, God appears to Jacob and reaffirms the promises He made to Abraham and Isaac, and now him. Then Jacob finally goes home to his father Isaac and sees him before he passes away. When Isaac dies at the age of 180 years, both Jacob and Esau are there to bury him.[16]

Wow! A lot happened in that 80 to 100 years of history: Lots of deception, mistrust, cheating, rape, murder and striving, enough material for a major soap opera to run daily for years! Who did all of this? It wasn't God. Don't blame Him for it. People did these things. "People ruin their lives by their own foolishness, and then are angry at the Lord."[17] However, one thing stands out to me as I review this part of history: God didn't abandon them. Rather, God kept His promises, encouraging them when they needed it and intervening to guide them and protect them when they were threatened.

I was especially intrigued with the wrestling match between Jacob and God. Who would have seen that one coming? God would really wrestle with a man, and that man would win? Really? Does that sound like what you think of God? Let's look at this a little closer, and maybe we can get to know our God more through this:

> During the night Jacob got up and took his two wives, his two servant wives, and his eleven sons and crossed the Jabbok River

with them. After taking them to the other side, he sent over all his possessions. This left Jacob all alone in the camp, and a man came and wrestled with him until the dawn began to break. When the man saw that he would not win the match, he touched Jacob's hip and wrenched it out of its socket. Then the man said, "Let me go, for the dawn is breaking!" But Jacob said, "I will not let you go unless you bless me." "What is your name?" the man asked. He replied, "Jacob." "Your name will no longer be Jacob," the man told him. "From now on you will be called Israel, because you have fought with God and with men and have won." "Please tell me your name," Jacob said. "Why do you want to know my name?" the man replied. Then he blessed Jacob there. Jacob named the place Peniel (which means "face of God"), for he said, "I have seen God face to face, yet my life has been spared." The sun was rising as Jacob left Peniel, and he was limping because of the injury to his hip. (Even today the people of Israel don't eat the tendon near the hip socket because of what happened that night when the man strained the tendon of Jacob's hip.) (Genesis 32:22–32, NLT).

An argument could be made that it really wasn't God that wrestled with Jacob. We need to resolve this before we go any further. If it was God that Jacob wrestled, then we can include what God does here in our evidence of what God is really like. If it was not God, then we don't want the actions of someone else to influence our perspective of God.

This passage of scripture uses "man" seven times to describe the person Jacob was wrestling. So, then it must have been a man, right? Not so fast. Jacob at first may have thought it was a man, but after the encounter with the "man" he concludes that it wasn't just a man he had been wrestling. He states, "For I have seen God face to face, and yet my life has been delivered."[18] He even names the place with a word that means "face of God." So, Jacob obviously thought it was God who he had just wrestled with. Note that this passage of scripture does not later say that Jacob was mistaken. Therefore, it could be implied that the writer of the book of Genesis thought Jacob was correct in what he had concluded. Nor does any other later part of the Bible say that Jacob was mistaken. So, at this point, Jacob, the author of Genesis, and the many authors of the rest of the Bible believe it was God who wrestled with Jacob.

But what made Jacob conclude this was God he had wrestled with? Let's look even closer at the surroundings of this event:

In the first verse of this chapter, we read "the angels of God met him."[19] The Bible doesn't say how Jacob knew they were angels. He had seen angels before in his dream at Bethel where God clearly spoke to him the same things God had spoken to his father Isaac and grandfather Abraham.[20] Perhaps these angels looked like the ones he had seen in his dream? We aren't sure, but he thought they were angels, so let's go with that because it doesn't matter except that it helps explain why he asks for a blessing during this wrestling match.

I don't believe Jacob would ask any stranger for a blessing. And I especially don't think he would wrestle a stranger for hours for a blessing. If the stranger ended up being poor or otherwise not blessed, then how could they bestow a blessing on Jacob who was already quite wealthy and otherwise blessed? How would this blessing help him with the meeting with his brother Esau and his four hundred men tomorrow?

I do believe Jacob would ask for a blessing from someone who he believed was greater than himself, whose blessing would improve Jacob's position in life from where it was then or would help him face his brother Esau tomorrow. The person doing the blessing needs to be greater, richer, or otherwise better than the one being blessed.[21]

Jacob had received a blessing years ago from his father Isaac (who would have been considered greater than him in that culture), but I don't find any other place in the Bible where Jacob was blessed by someone up to this point in time.

So, it's my hunch that Jacob started asking for a blessing once he thought the man who came to him may be an angel. Perhaps that's what started the wrestling match. I could hear Jacob or the man saying, "I'll wrestle you for it!" A blessing received from an angel would be worth something! That is why I believe he refused to let his wrestling opponent go unless he received a blessing.

His opponent was either getting weary from wrestling or needed to get out of there. I believe it is the latter, under the assumption that the darkness hid His true identity, which He couldn't let be revealed as daylight approached. So, his opponent "touched" Jacob's hip, and it went out of socket.

Have you ever had a hip out of socket? Someone I knew who played football had a dislocated hip, and he had to be carried off the field on a stretcher and was in a tremendous amount of pain. For Jacob to continue to wrestle and hold on to his opponent after having a hip out of socket is downright amazing. I would have quit, tapped out, cried "uncle" or done whatever I could to quit the wrestling match immediately and tend to my injury. But not Jacob! He wanted that blessing from this angel!

That was Jacob. He didn't let go of his opponent, whoever it was. His first match was with his older brother Esau. He wrestled with his brother Esau in his mother's womb[22], and he held on for dear life to Esau's heel when he and his brother were born.[23] I would agree with those who think Jacob continued to wrestle with Esau throughout their time living with their parents, and even later in life.[24] He held on to Rachel when Laban tricked him and gave him Leah instead for his wife, agreeing to work another seven years for Rachel rather than giving up and going home.[25] After those 14 years were over, he continued to endure Laban's trickery and hold on despite Laban changing his wages 10 times, until God finally did tell him to let go and go home.[26] I see the tenacity and fighting spirit in Jacob that makes him hold on to this angel until he gets his blessing.

Keep in mind that this wrestling match was at night. This was not like our wrestling matches today. There were no stadium or arena lights to help Jacob see what his opponent may have been doing. They may have been wrestling in utter darkness. Their only light may have been from a campfire. But unless they took scheduled breaks in this wrestling match, they would not have been able to keep the fire burning. Jacob probably would not have agreed to taking scheduled breaks because his opponent may have left the scene just as mysteriously as He had arrived. There may have been some moonlight, but even that might have been blocked by trees or the surrounding mountains.

Would you want to wrestle a stranger in the darkness? Not me, unless I was confident that I was better than my opponent, because I couldn't see what my opponent was trying to do to me until it was too late. However, if your strategy is to hold on to your opponent until they give up, regardless of what they do to you, then maybe you can win in a wrestling match in the dark. Such is Jacob!

Jacob still had hold of his opponent and had persevered. He was finally going to get his blessing. But first, his opponent asked him his name. Jacob complied and told him his name. Then his opponent told him something that is amazing, "Your name will no longer be Jacob. From now on you will be called Israel, because you have *fought with God* and with men and have won."[27] Jacob asked his opponent's name, not yet realizing the magnitude of what has just been said to him. However, his opponent didn't comply in sharing His name, but then blessed him.

I wish we knew what words were used in that blessing! However, perhaps that is not as important to Jacob later as what Jacob had already been told. Since Jacob had received his blessing, he released his hold on his opponent, watched his opponent walk off into the pre-dawn darkness, winced some from the pain of his hip, and rested. While resting, his mind continued to dwell on the wrestling match and then on the conversation and the words spoken to him a few moments earlier. Then, I believe it hit him. When had he ever fought with God?! He searched his memories like someone frantically flipping through a box of pictures and doesn't recall ever fighting with God. He asked himself, "Was that God I just wrestled?" He thought some more and concluded that it was. He named the place Peniel (face of God) because he had seen God face to face and yet not died.

Some time passed, and Jacob moved to Shechem and then back to Bethel where God appeared to him in a dream when he first fled from Esau. God appeared to him again at Bethel. The text does not say whether in a dream, vision, or in the form of a man. But God told him again the same thing Jacob was told right before he released his hold on his wrestling opponent, "'Your name is Jacob, but you will not be called Jacob any longer. From now on your name will be Israel.' So God renamed him Israel."[28] I believe, in Jacob's mind, this confirmed to him it was God who wrestled with him.

This isn't the only time in the Bible someone saw a man and concluded then or later that it was God they were talking to. We read earlier in Genesis where Abraham was visited by three men, two of them ended up being angels, and one of them was the Lord.[29] Joshua also encountered a man near Jericho before the siege of that city began. This man said He was the "Commander of the army of the Lord", and Joshua fell on his face and worshipped Him. Unlike angels or holy men who refused worship,[30] Joshua's worship was not refused. Instead, Joshua was told to take off his shoes for he was on holy ground.[31] Manoah, the father of Samson, and his wife had a similar experience, thinking they were talking to a man and then when the man ascended into heaven, believed that they had "seen God."[32] Like Jacob's encounter, the "man" declined to give His name to Manoah.[33] However, I don't recall any angel in the Bible refusing to share their name with the people to whom they were speaking.[34] So, I am choosing to believe Jacob's report that he had wrestled with God.

That question resolved, I am still left with two other major questions:

1. Why would God wrestle with Jacob?
2. How could Jacob win a wrestling match with God?

Let's start with the first question. Why would God wrestle with Jacob? Why wouldn't God just make a proclamation to him, as He had done in the past, or speak to him in a dream? Why wrestle? We hadn't seen where God in bodily form wrestled with someone prior to this, nor will we see this in the rest of the Bible. What was God hoping to accomplish by wrestling with Jacob?

What attributes of God do we know about that could provide an answer for us? Well, we know God is "merciful and gracious, long-suffering and abundant in goodness and truth" because He said that about Himself to Moses.[35] In addition, Jesus referred to Him not only as His Father, but our Father.[36] He also said that God the Father loves us.[37] So, picturing our God as a loving Father who wanted to speak love and truth to Jacob in a special way, how does that help us answer the question of why God would stoop from His heavenly throne to wrestle with Jacob, who was probably sweaty and stinky after traveling in a hot climate for days?

I believe God wanted to speak to Jacob in a language he would understand, not just with his ears, but with his heart and all his physical faculties. Jacob likely had been holding onto or wrestling with people all his life. Esau, because of his love for the outdoors, was probably stronger than Jacob and probably won most of their childhood matches. This is probably the reason Jacob feared Esau's wrath after Jacob took both his birthright and his father's blessing. Jacob probably wasn't the best wrestler, but he might have learned that if he was going to survive, he had to outlast the other person by sheer determination, learning lessons from each of his defeats that he could take to the next struggle, steadily improving and consistently willing to take more punishment than he could dish out in order to prevail. I believe God, in an act of love and like an earthly Father, would wrestle with him, not wrestling with all His power, but just enough to give Jacob a struggle and in the end, let Jacob win.

I'm sure I'm not the only earthly dad who has wrestled his kids and played against them in basketball or other athletic contests. A good father will hold back most of their strength and ability in order to let their child have a good chance of winning, to make a good struggle out of what would normally be a lopsided contest. Sometimes the father lets the child win because if the child never wins, they can get discouraged and quit. So, the father or mother must balance between their child losing so much that they get discouraged and letting their child win so much that they become arrogant and don't strive to improve because they always win against their parents.

To me, God was doing just that with Jacob. He was then, is now, and will always be Almighty God. He could have annihilated Jacob in a millisecond if He had wanted to, but instead He struggled with Jacob for hours, testing him and perhaps even enjoying the interaction He was having with His child. And then, in an act of love, He touches Jacob's hip, knocking it out of socket and creating tremendous pain for Jacob, right before giving up and declaring Jacob the winner.

If God didn't know Jacob completely, He would have been taking a tremendous risk in touching Jacob's hip and knocking it out of socket. Jacob could have easily given up at that point and consoled himself by thinking he had done well wrestling that long with an angel. But God knew Jacob and knew he still wouldn't give up. After much reflection on this nighttime wrestling match, now every time Jacob walked with his limp, it reminded him he had wrestled with God who said he had prevailed. This gave Jacob both great confidence in all his dealings after having been affirmed by Almighty God and yet great humility and reverence for God in knowing that as easily as God touched his hip, He could have done that from the beginning of the match and easily destroyed Jacob if He had wanted. He now realized God had held back. You don't hold back for people you don't love, so he now realized how much God must love him.

One important point I need to make here before we continue. Even though God was going to let Jacob win this wrestling match, could that have happened if Jacob had not at least tried? What if Jacob had thought something like, "There's no way I have any chance wrestling an angel. I'm not doing it!" If Jacob had not even tried, God would not have been able to give him the victory.

We have answered the two questions, "Why would God wrestle with Jacob?" and "How could Jacob win a wrestling match with God?" Both answers revolved around God showing love to Jacob.

Now, one more question. What does all this tell us about God the Father? Pray and think about this for a minute, and after you've done that, review a few possibilities I have listed for you:

1. God knows that because we love Him, we are going to encounter a lot of resistance in this world, because the world hates Him, and so it will hate us too.[38] That's why we need persistence and resolve to hold onto God, not letting go of Him by faith and in prayer in order to hold on despite the resistance the world will bring us.

2. God may sometimes feel like an adversary to us. His objective is to make us better, not hurt us. I've heard it said that God is not interested in making us happy as much as He is in making us holy [like Him]. Much like when a sports team practices, they play against themselves. In football, that means a teammate tackling another teammate so that the whole team will become better. In the same way, God may tackle us or wrestle with us, with the goal of making us better. Read Hebrews 12:1–11 for more insight.

3. God values persistence. A parable Jesus told His disciples demonstrates this beautifully:

One day Jesus told his disciples a story to show that they should always pray and never give up. "There was a judge in a certain city," he said, "who neither feared God nor cared about people. A widow of that city came to him repeatedly, saying, 'Give me justice in this dispute with my enemy.' The judge ignored her for a while, but finally he said to himself, 'I don't fear God or care about people, but this woman is driving me crazy. I'm going to see that she gets justice, because she is wearing me out with her constant requests!'"

Then the Lord said, "Learn a lesson from this unjust judge. Even he rendered a just decision in the end. So don't you think God will surely give justice to his chosen people who cry out to him day and night? Will he keep putting them off? I tell you, he will grant justice to them quickly! But when the Son of Man returns, how many will he find on the earth who have faith?" (Luke 18:1–8, NLT, italics added for emphasis).

Let's resolve to do all we can to hold on to God. Nigel Briggs wrote a beautiful and memorable song with this theme called, "I Will Hold On":[39] We sing it at my church. The last phrase of the chorus ends with, "I will hold on, yes, I will trust in You." Let's hold on by trusting God.

CHAPTER 15
GENESIS 37–50: WORKING ALL THINGS TOGETHER

The remainder of Genesis focuses primarily on the lives of Jacob and Joseph. At first glance, there doesn't appear to be much to learn about God in these chapters. However, follow me for a few paragraphs as we set the stage to discover some marvelous truths about Him.

Chapter 37 begins by discussing Jacob's family, especially his son Joseph. There is trouble on the horizon for this family and, as with most family dynamics, its origins go back to some previous circumstances that had negative impacts on some of the family that were never fully resolved. If you will recall from Genesis 29 and 30, Jacob had two wives. He was tricked into marrying his first wife Leah in place of the woman he greatly loved. His second wife Rachel was the one he intended to marry in the first place. These two wives were sisters too, so any sibling rivalries between them before they were married probably only became stronger after marriage.

God saw that Leah was not loved by Jacob, so He blessed her with children.[1] She had several children while Rachel remained childless.

Rachel became jealous of Leah and gave Jacob her servant Billah as a wife to bear children since it seemed Rachel could not have any. What a strange thing to do. This is an example of how jealousy will make you do unusual things! Billah had two sons fathered by Jacob. Rachel took great delight in this, even saying, "I have had a great struggle with my sister, and I have won."[2]

Predictably, the rivalry between Leah and Rachel grew. Leah, fearing she had stopped having children, struck back by giving her servant Zilpah as a wife to Jacob and Zilpah bore two more sons to Jacob. Then, Leah started having children again and had two more sons and a daughter. When it appeared that Jacob was done fathering children, "then God remembered Rachel; He listened to her and enabled her to conceive."[3] She finally had two children, Joseph and (after Jacob had returned to the land of Canaan), Benjamin. Rachel died while giving birth to Benjamin.

It was against this backdrop of sibling rivalry that Joseph and his brothers were born and grew up. Their mothers (at least two and probably four if you include the two servants who bore children to Jacob) fought for Jacob's love and attention. I am confident this rivalry was passed down to their children. I have no doubt this rivalry kept the family dynamics at a constant boil, fueling even more family strife than what is recorded in the Genesis text. So, it should not be surprising that when Jacob gives Joseph a "robe of many colors,"[4] this act of love expressed to Joseph resulted in even more family rivalry and hatred. Joseph's older brothers, all from different moms than Joseph, hated Joseph as a result "and could not speak peacefully to him."[5]

I've wondered why Jacob would give such a gift to only Joseph. Wouldn't he be aware of the conflicts already existing in his family and realize how this would make things even worse? Didn't he care? We don't know. It's possible Jacob's reasoning was well thought through and justified the trouble it caused. It could have been that Jacob, with good intentions tried to do something good to improve a situation that ended up causing more problems. At that time,

Rachel, Joseph's mother, was dead. Perhaps Jacob gave the gift as an attempt to make up for the loss Joseph was feeling for his mom as Jacob realized Joseph now felt very alone amidst a hostile and dysfunctional family?

We won't know the reasoning this side of heaven. But it is sometimes helpful to know that people whom God chose to bless and use in the Bible had some of the same junk in their family lives as we do in ours today. Your family situation and related dynamics are not too difficult for God! He is amazing at taking what we might consider broken and dysfunctional and turning them into beautiful things, if we are willing to trust Him enough to change our ways to His way and wait patiently on Him.

If you haven't yet read the chapters in Genesis which I am reviewing, I strongly recommend it. My brief summarization that precedes and follows this paragraph will leave out many details that lend color to the string of events to come.

Continuing the story, Joseph's brother's hatred of him came to a head. They faked Joseph's death and sold him into slavery, and Joseph was transported to Egypt. I'm sure he felt for the next several months that God had abandoned him. However, God gave him such success and favor with his Egyptian master that his master turned over control of everything he possessed to Joseph. Joseph probably felt God was with him again.

Unfortunately, Joseph's master's wife wanted him to sleep with her, and when Joseph refused so that he didn't sin against God, she falsely accused him of attempting to rape her. Joseph was then thrown into prison. How scary and unpleasant that must have been for Joseph! He had been falsely accused and was being punished in prison in a strange land all by himself. Do you think he wondered, "God, where are you and why are you allowing all this to happen to me?" I would have.

But God never left him, even though it may have felt to Joseph like he had been abandoned by God. While in that Egyptian prison for at least two years and probably closer to five or even 10, the Bible says God gave him favor with the prison warden, who put him in charge of the entire prison. Then, through a series of dramatic events that you must read for yourself to comprehend, Joseph was taken from the prison and became the leader of all Egypt, subject only to the king of Egypt. Wow! Talk about a major "upside down" as stated in Chapter 13, bouncing from the lowest of lows to the highest of highs, Joseph certainly experienced that. Twice!

His father, brothers and their families eventually went to Egypt to avoid death by famine and are reunited with Joseph. Joseph provided for them, and they lived in Egypt. Then their father Jacob died, and his brothers feared Joseph will finally take his revenge against them for selling him into slavery. Certain that revenge was coming, his brothers sent a message to Joseph asking him to forgive them, implying that their father Jacob had wanted that, and then they came to him and fell on their faces before him saying they are his slaves!

How Joseph responded to his brothers is amazing. Having recognized God's role in how they mistreated him, Joseph said, "Do not fear, for am I in the place of God? As for you, you meant evil against me, but God meant it for good, to bring it about that many people should be kept alive, as they are today. So do not fear; I will provide for you and your little ones."[6]

When Joseph said that God worked things out to keep many people alive, he wasn't just referring to his family. Through Joseph's actions in Egypt, food had been saved up in Egypt during the seven years of abundance to keep the people of Egypt and the surrounding lands from starving during the seven-year drought.

God had taken the hatred of Joseph's brothers and used it to save not only those brothers, but also a good portion of the population of the earth. Isn't it amazing that God can take bad things such as the hatred of others and work them out to ultimately produce good things?

That might be great if you are one of those who were saved from famine. However, it was probably not that good if you were the one who had to be hated, treated terribly, beaten, abandoned, sold into slavery, falsely accused, put into prison and left alone from family and friends for years! Couldn't God just as easily have told the Egyptians to go find Joseph and pay him a lot of money to work in Egypt for a while? Maybe, but that would have required the people of Egypt to *believe God and obey Him* when He spoke to them to elevate someone of a race and occupation they despised to reign over them.[7] Let's be real. That's wasn't going to happen. So, God chose to work around the hatred, discrimination and pride of people who had a free will and wicked hearts in order to rescue people. That's what God did by bringing Joseph to Egypt through much adversity.

> Isn't it amazing that God can take bad things such as the hatred of others and work them out to ultimately produce good things?

Joseph was not the only one to suffer great hardship to be used by God to help other people. That's also what God has done with many others in history and is also doing this with many people around the globe today. Maybe you are or soon will be one of them.

I believe God is desperately trying to get people to hear and believe His message. He doesn't want to send them away to hell forever. Just like with Joseph, God is trying to save a lot of people from dying, both in this life and for eternity. He sometimes allows our lives to go in directions we don't want so that others can be presented with that message. Even if people won't believe Him, He must try. We are all His children, and He doesn't want to see us die an eternal death that was intended for the devil and his angels, not us.[8] Like Joseph, that can mean we might be wronged and suffer ill treatment, false accusations and imprisonment. Like Jesus and others who have followed Him, that can mean suffering even to the point of death on this earth to get God's message to those who need it.

How about you? Are you suffering? There is a lot of suffering in this world. Most of it has been caused by humankind, not by God. A verse from the book of Proverbs says it well, "People ruin their lives by their own foolishness, and then are angry at the Lord."[9] You may be suffering as a result of your own or someone else's foolishness, and it has nothing to do with God using it to reach other people. If your suffering is self-inflicted, it might end if you turn to the Lord. See Appendix A for help on how to turn to the Lord. In this case, suffering is probably being used to turn you away from something and draw you to God. So, suffering can produce a good result.

In case you are indeed suffering for the kingdom of God, be encouraged. Suffering is producing a good result in this case too. Jesus Himself said, "God blesses you when people mock you and persecute you and lie about you and say all sorts of evil things against you because you are my followers. Be happy about it! Be very glad! For a great reward awaits you in heaven. And remember, the ancient prophets were persecuted in the same way."[10]

So, whether suffering is caused by your own actions, by the family dynamics into which you were born, for the benefit of God's kingdom or for some other reason that only God may know, God can work suffering and difficulties together for good.

- It was true in the life of Joseph.
- It was true for the Apostle Paul who wrote in his letter to the Romans, "And we know that for those who love God all things work together for good, for those who are called according to his purpose."[11] Paul was eventually killed for his faith.
- It is true for Christians all over the world who are suffering persecution and even being killed for their faith in Christ today.
- And it is true for you! God is working your difficulties for good too.

CHAPTER 16
JUDAH: FROM WICKEDNESS TO THE HEART OF JESUS

Before we finish with the book of Genesis, I must point out one more thing inside the book of Genesis that you've got to see. It's beautiful! I had never been aware of this particular transformation until I saw it while writing this book.

Judah was one of the 12 sons of Jacob. Early in his life, he may have been a fairly wicked man. When his brothers wanted to kill their half-brother Joseph, it was Judah's idea to instead sell him as a slave. Genesis 38 reads that after Joseph was sold into slavery, Judah left his brothers for a while and lived with the ungodly inhabitants of the land, marrying a Canaanite woman. He had three sons with her. Two of these sons would later be killed by the Lord for their wickedness. While it is possible Judah could have been a good man who, despite his best efforts, raised wicked sons, it is more likely that he also had wicked tendencies which, when mixed with the pagan beliefs from his wife's family, multiplied in the lives of his sons. There is an old proverb, "The apple doesn't fall too far from the tree," meaning a child is a lot like their parent. That was probably the case with Judah and his sons.

Genesis 42 tells us that when Jacob sent his sons to Egypt to buy grain, Judah was one of them. Over time, Judah must have returned to his father's family or at least lived close by. Perhaps the widespread famine had forced Judah to return to be with or near Jacob, like in Jesus's parable of the prodigal son.[1] This is only speculation on my part. Regardless of how it happened, Judah was now back in the presence of his father, Jacob. He couldn't help but witness the grief that his father felt as his father believed Joseph was killed by a wild animal, a lie Judah and his brothers had told their father after they sold Judah into slavery.

Perhaps seeing the initial grief of his father over the loss of Joseph is what pushed Judah to leave his father and brothers to go live with the pagan inhabitants of the land originally. Living with strangers may have been easier than living with a grieving father and a guilty conscience, knowing he was the cause of his father's grief. He may have tried to get away from this, but circumstances pushed him back into his father's presence to hear his father's grief again.

Upon this backdrop, let's now look at what happens as Judah and his brothers went to Egypt to buy grain. Benjamin didn't make the trip to Egypt with the others because Jacob can't bear the thought of potentially losing his only other son from his beloved wife Rachel, who was dead. When they arrived, they were brought to the governor of the land, who is their brother Joseph! However, they didn't recognize him, as it had been at least 20 years since they sold him into slavery. Joseph recognized them but did not let anyone know. The Bible doesn't tell us why Joseph requested that Benjamin, the only other one of his brothers to be born to his mom, be brought to Egypt. I can only speculate that Joseph wanted to see that his half-brothers hadn't also harmed Benjamin before Joseph revealed who he was to his brothers. Regardless, when the brothers returned to their father Jacob and told him about this request for Benjamin to be brought to Egypt, Jacob recalled the memories of losing Joseph. At first, Jacob refused to let Benjamin go to Egypt.

Being forced between taking Benjamin to Egypt or starvation,[2] Judah and his brothers pursued Jacob about releasing Benjamin into their care for a return trip to Egypt. Jacob had told them earlier, "If harm comes to him on the journey you are taking, you will bring my gray head down to the grave in sorrow."[3] Finally, Jacob allowed Benjamin to go, but only after Judah told him, "I myself will guarantee his safety; you can hold me personally responsible for him. If I do not bring him back to you and set him here before you, I will bear the blame before you all my life."[4]

Judah and his brothers returned to Egypt, this time with Benjamin. Things go well at first, but then the Egyptian governor (Joseph) insisted Benjamin remain in Egypt in prison while all the others returned with the food needed for the survival of their families.

It was at this point in the story that Judah demonstrated the transformation that had taken place in his heart, from wickedness to what I believe is the heart of Jesus. He pleaded for Benjamin to be released to return to his father and for himself to take Benjamin's place to remain Joseph's slave. He ended his appeal by saying, "Now then, please let your servant remain here as my lord's slave in place of the boy, and let the boy return with his brothers. How can I go back to my father if the boy is not with me? No! Do not let me see the misery that would come on my father."[5]

In Judah's transformation, he went from someone who had hated his brother and sold him into slavery to someone who would voluntarily become a slave to return his brother back to his father. What a change! This caused Joseph to experience such emotion that he wept; and, then he finally revealed himself to his brothers.[6]

What do you think caused such a huge transformation in Judah? Remember that Judah had years earlier suffered the loss of two of his sons. To me, his grief from that loss helped him understand the severe grief of his father from the loss of Joseph.

You may also wonder why I now see the heart of Jesus in Judah. I see it when he begged to take the place of his brother in slavery so that his brother could return to his father. That is essentially what Jesus did for us on the cross. We should have been on that cross suffering for our sins, not Jesus. We should have experienced separation from our Heavenly Father for our sins. However, Jesus took our place and suffered what we should have suffered so that we could be returned to our Heavenly Father. On the night before Jesus was crucified for us, Jesus prayed and asked if there was any way He could avoid dying for us. He knew what suffering was in store for Him. He knew that His eternal relationship with His Father God would be interrupted, as the sins of all the world would be placed on Him to bear. But, with a greater passion than the pain and anguish He would experience in the next 24 hours, He so wanted to obey His father. He, like Judah, could say, "How can I go back to my father if the boy [us] is not with me [not able to go to God]?" So, Jesus willingly took our place of punishment so that we could return to God.

In this short story from Genesis 44:33–34, Jacob played a role like God the Father, Judah played a role like Jesus, and Benjamin played a role like us. Since the book you're reading is about God the Father, I want you to look at the emotion Jacob had for Benjamin, his son. This is how our Heavenly Father feels about you. You may think God is looking at you now with eyes of scorn, or even hatred, but you are wrong! Jesus said that He was the only one who truly knows His Father,[7] and He revealed the Father's heart toward us by telling the story of the prodigal son.[8] In this story, the father, who upon seeing his wayward child, was filled with compassion and, didn't walk but ran to his child, threw his arms around his child and kissed him. That is how God feels, no, yearns to be with you, if you will only return to Him and let Him.

Will you?

PART TWO
PERSONAL STORIES

CHAPTER 17
A LOPSIDED GAME

Years ago, my wife and I were hosting a lot of people in our house for one of the holidays. My kids were in their pre-teen years and as kids, would rather play outside than stay in the house all day visiting with adults. Fortunately, it was a nice day outside, so some of the kids had gone outside to play and enjoy the nice weather. After a while, I decided to go outside and check on them to see that everything was OK.

I saw that my son and two other boys who lived near us were playing basketball in our driveway. I greeted the other boys and asked them how they were doing. After a few more questions, I realized I was interrupting their game of basketball. But since I had played basketball with them in the past, they invited me to join their game in progress. Since it was two against one at that moment, by me joining the game, it would be two against two, which was fairer. I was then surprised to find out that the two neighbor boys, who were taller and older than my son, had been on one team, and my son was the other team!

That didn't quite seem right to me. That's not usually how you would divide three people up on two teams if you had three people playing. You'd probably pick the tallest to be on one team and the other two on the other team, or maybe the tallest and shortest as one team against the third person, but probably not the two tallest on one team and the shortest on the other team by himself. It wasn't surprising that the score was 8–0 (my son had 0) and they were playing to 10. One more basket and my son would lose, and the other team would win. Rather than start over with a new game, they wanted to finish this game and for me to join my son and be on his team.

"OK, I'll play," I said. These guys were 10 to 12 years old. But me, I'm in my 40s, six foot two inches tall and played a couple years of high school basketball. We played. With a little hard play on my part, we made the score 8–2, then 8–4, then 8–6, and finally tied the game at 8–8. They had the ball, but with some good defense and good fortune, they were not making their baskets, so I got the ball back from them. The score was tied 8–8, and we had the ball.

I had made all four baskets, so they were both on me like fleas on a dog trying to keep me from making the winning basket. I knew I could make the next basket and win the game for my son and me, but I saw my son open in the corner. It was a long shot from where he was at, but he was wide open and wanted me to pass the ball to him. If he missed, they could win, but if he could make this long shot, we would win. So, I passed the ball to him. He shot! Nothing but net! What a shot! We won! I was elated and high-fived my son!

The boys wanted to play another game, but I told them I had to get back inside with the other folks. I walked back into the house with a great joy inside of me that my son, with my help, won a game that normally he would have lost. I didn't hear an audible voice, but my mind was instantly filled with what I believe to be the Lord's words: "That joy you're feeling after helping your son win his game … that's what I feel like when I help you win."

When I played basketball in high school, my team wasn't great, but we won a few games. However, I never felt the joy of winning then like I did when my son made the winning basket that afternoon. It was hitting me now: How I felt is how God feels when He does something with us.

> **How I felt is how God feels when He does something with us.**

I could have played both neighbor boys and won all by myself without my son, but that wouldn't have been any fun. It wouldn't have been a fair game, as I was so much older and bigger than they were. Where is the joy in that?

In the same way, I feel God could whip Satan and all of His enemies with His proverbial "arms tied behind His back." He doesn't need any help from us. If we had any spiritual power of our own to do anything to help God, He wouldn't need it. He chooses to involve us, those of us who are His children through accepting and following Jesus, so that we can do something with Him. Doing something with God is how we learn to know Him. And what joy it must bring Him to see us, armed with only our faith in His promises, defeat His foe. His weak, flesh and blood children can whip up on His powerful spiritual enemy by relying on His promises.

Yes, God wants to help us win against the enemy. Don't get tricked into thinking that this means God will always help you win in competitions with other people in sports, business or other facets of this earthly life. If I had two sons playing basketball against each other on the driveway that day, my actions and my feelings afterward would have been a lot different. But believe me, God wants you to win in any and every spiritual battle you face with His enemy.

People sometimes ask, "After Jesus's resurrection, why didn't Jesus show Himself to the whole world?" They are essentially asking, "Why didn't God take the shot to make the winning basket?" That is a very logical question to ask. However, they don't understand that God knows He can win things easily by Himself, but He wants to experience the joy of being in the battle with His children and seeing them making the shot and winning the contest. They may not make the shot the first time, but I believe He is there to get the rebound and then pass the ball back to them to try again.

People also sometimes ask, "If God is so powerful and loving, why doesn't He come down here and fix everything that's wrong?" Again, they are essentially asking, "Why doesn't God take the ball, make the shot and win the game for us?" They don't realize that God wants us to take the winning shot.

I never would have thought this way if God had not opened my eyes to this idea the day after the game on the driveway with my son. Likewise, I now picture God being so proud of His children, when they remain faithful while they are being "re-educated" by Communists in a cold and muddy prison somewhere in Asia or being interrogated and beaten in a small and hot jail in the Middle East, keeping their belief in Jesus under such cruel conditions. In some cases, even winning others to Christ by their willingness to suffer under such harsh conditions and not denying the Lord. With no weapons, money or other instruments of this world, they remain faithful to Christ even unto death. Under such awful circumstances, they are winning the contest, defeating the enemies of our God, and their Heavenly Father is so proud of them.

God wants to be with you and help you do things with Him. He wants you to know Him by working together in the great contest of life on this earth. Do you realize that? Are you making yourself available to be with Him? Pray and ask the Lord what you should do to be more available to Him. What does He want you to do or where does He want you to go so that He can pass you the ball so you can make the winning shot? He and all of Heaven are waiting to celebrate your winning life lived with Him.

If he's already passed you the ball, what are you going to do with it? Hold it out of fear? Just keep dribbling it because of uncertainty or unbelief? Or shoot it?

Thank you, God, for loving us so much and allowing us the opportunity to know you by experiencing life with you. Thank you for throwing us the ball!

CHAPTER 18
MUCH MORE THAN PUPPY LOVE

When our kids reached a certain age, they began to ask us to get a puppy. They had friends who had dogs and so our kids wanted one of their own. After a month or more of give-and-take on who would do what as far as daily chores to take care of the dog, I started the search to find just the right dog. I did research to find the right breed for kids and discussed it with the family to came up with the type of dog to get. I then found a breeder with a puppy who met the description and loaded up the kids in the car to pick up the puppy.

The puppy was about twelve weeks old when we brought it home. Everything was going great on that first day until it was time for the kids to go to bed. The puppy didn't understand why all the attention it had been receiving was now gone. Then all the whimpering (puppy crying) started, and it was keeping the kids awake. So, I got involved to give the puppy some attention to keep the puppy from breaking down the family schedule and so the kids could get some sleep since tomorrow was a school day.

This was my first dog as an adult. I thought this was going to be easy. I quickly realized that I must not have understood all that my parents had done to have a dog for me as a kid. Whereas my dogs growing up were mostly dogs that stayed outside, this new puppy was going to be able to be in the house, so it could play with the kids all the time. Having the dog inside added a further degree of difficulty that I had not fully envisioned.

As an amateur at raising a dog, I made some bad mistakes. I made them for the right reasons, but they were still mistakes. That first night, in order to keep the dog quiet and to be aware of when it needed to go outside, I had the dog sleep beside my bed on the floor. I laid on my stomach and let my right arm hang over the edge of the bed so that I could pet it if it felt alone and scared. I was somehow able to get some sleep for just a few short minutes here and there, but at least I kept it quiet so not to wake the rest of the family. I also succeeded in it not having any accidents in the house through the night.

The routine continued for a few nights and things gradually got better. Unfortunately, I didn't realize that all I had been doing to keep this dog happy was spoiling it while at the same time allowing it to capture my heart. While it would sleep in the kids' room some as we had hoped, its favorite place to sleep was right by me on the floor when I was in bed. This dog had morphed from a dog that was intended for the kids into a dog that was mainly mine that I shared with the rest of the family.

We did have some great times with it. We developed some games in the house that we played with it that were fun for both us and the dog. There was one in particular that we called "hall ball." We would laugh so hard and all of us, including the dog, seemed to enjoy it. It made for some great video camera footage during our kids' childhood years.

Eventually, the dog's allegiance and affection for me was starting to become a problem. As we analyzed things, we were seeing that it recognized me as the alpha male of our "pack," and it was vying for my attention. It had become jealous of my wife. We didn't know what to do about it and hoped it would resolve itself on its own, but it didn't. Then there were a couple instances where it got jealous of my wife and growled at her while she was working in the kitchen sweeping the floor. Then things steadily progressed and got worse when it nipped at her in the kitchen.

This was now a problem, and I didn't know what to do. This was a beloved member of our family now. We had spent several years together at this point. Not only was this dog a big part of my kids' life, it had become a part of my life too.

Then what we feared would happen occurred. My wife, while leaving for work very early one morning before I or the kids were awake, walked over to my side of the bed to give me a kiss goodbye and to let me know she was leaving to go to work as she had done many times over the years. However, this time the dog was lying in the dark beside my bed, and my wife didn't see him there. When she leaned over to kiss me, the dog lunged at her and clamped down on her hand with his teeth and then held on for what seemed like an eternity, although it was probably only one to two seconds. I woke up right before this happened, expecting a favorite kiss from my beloved and saw the whole thing happen. What a nightmare.

My wife was screaming in pain. Fortunately, her car keys were in the hand that was bit. The car keys kept the dog's bottom teeth from coming up into her hand. Otherwise, rather than just having puncture wounds on top of the hand to deal with, there could have been major damage to her tendons, ligaments and bones.

We were all in a state of shock for a few days. All of us except for our dog. He behaved with me as though nothing had ever happened. But we couldn't undo what had been done. The thought of this happening again was hard to think about. What if one of my kids ran to our bed in the middle of the night and this happened again? It was obvious we could not keep him. It also became apparent after talking with others that we could not give him to another home knowing that he had bitten someone so badly. So, I made the decision to have him put down.

This was hard to do. I'd never had to do this before. It wasn't like I was putting down some unknown animal. I was putting down someone I had consoled at night by sleeping with my hand lying over him. We had spent many hours on walks with him. We had laughed for hours playing with him. He would run to me when he was scared by something, and he kept me company when I was home alone. This was a friend that I was taking to the vet to have put down.

The vet assured me that I was doing the right thing. He offered to handle everything while I went back home, or I could stay. I chose to stay and held him as he went to sleep for good.

I don't remember if it was on the way home or after I got home, and I don't remember if I felt the Lord was talking to me or if the thought just popped into my own head, and I'm not sure that it matters. What did hit me was the sense of loss I had in having to put down a friend of my family, and my own friend, and wondering whether the Lord will feel this way when He has to send away from His presence forever someone that He loves so much.

I'd grown to love a dog just by taking care of it and spending time with it. That is nothing compared to all God has done for each of us in giving us life itself, seeing every move we make, hearing every thought, and enjoying the person He created "live and move and have our being."[1] And to top even that, He gave His son Jesus to die on a cross. All we have to do is believe Him enough to obey Him, and then none of us would have to be separated from Him forever. Yet, people won't take advantage of that, and God the Father will have His hand forced to send every one of them to an eternal death of separation from Him in the lake of fire. This lake of fire was created for Satan and his angels, not for the men and women God created to be with Him forever in heaven. But God will have to go through the heartache of sending His precious ones to this lake of fire in order to satisfy justice. We've seen God kill people in the Bible. However, that was only a death in their body and many of those that were killed may be with us for eternity in heaven. We've never seen God say an eternal goodbye to people as will be done at that great and final judgment day of the Lord.

The pain I believe God will feel in carrying out this final judgment on nonbelieving men and women reminds me of another story I heard a friend of mine once tell. He shared about one of his friends who had a dad who died. This dad went to his grave not ever turning to the Lord to accept His offer of forgiveness and embracing a life following Jesus. That dad's son, the friend of my friend, was so grieved that he would never see his dad in heaven that he cried and wept before the Lord about it. However, as he did this, it began to hit him how God loved his dad much more than he ever did. Once that began to sink in, the roles changed in this time of prayer. Instead of God consoling this man who had lost his dad forever, this man started trying to console the Lord for His loss of His child. Think of that! As much as we love other people, God loves them so much more. Doesn't it make sense then that He will feel much more anguish than us at losing them forever?

> **As much as we love other people, God loves them so much more.**

John 10:10 reads, "The thief comes only to steal and kill and destroy. I came that they may have life and have it abundantly." Every time I used to read that verse, I used to think about the thief (Satan) stealing from me or from other people. I had not ever thought about the thief stealing from the Lord until recently. And in one sense, the thief never steals directly from the Lord because he can't deceive or outwit the Lord. That is impossible. But in another sense, he does steal from the Lord indirectly in that he can steal things from God's children if we let him. In other words, Satan can suggest lies to us, which if we believe, can steal knowledge from us, knowledge of God's goodness. Without that knowledge, we may run from God instead of running to Him. In so doing, Satan can be said to have stolen us from God.

In 2 Peter 3:9 (NIV), it reads, "The Lord is not slow in keeping his promise, as some understand slowness. Instead He is patient with you, not wanting anyone to perish, but everyone to come to repentance." That verse means that if God got His way, no one would perish in hell, but everyone would believe and follow Jesus. However, God has given us a free will, which means we can choose whether we will obey God or not. The word "free" is not used in a financial sense as to mean it costs nothing, but rather in a sense of compulsion, in that we are free to do what we choose. Otherwise, if we had no free will, we would be His robots, not His children. The upside to giving us a free will is that we can choose to love God, not out of compulsion, but out of genuine love.

The downside to God giving us a free will is that we can choose not to obey Him. God wants us to choose to love Him, but the decision has been put into our hands. If we let ourselves be deceived and choose not to believe God and love and follow Him, then not only are we going to be stolen from, killed and destroyed (as stated in John 10:10), but God is going to suffer loss too in that it was His will that we believe and follow Jesus and live rather than be stolen from, killed and destroyed.

Revelation 21:4 is a famous verse from the Bible that reads, "He will wipe away every tear from their eyes, and death shall be no more, neither shall there be mourning, nor crying, nor pain anymore, for the former things have passed away." This is a verse that is typically shared with us when we are mourning to encourage us that things will get better. That is proper. However, one time I read Revelation Chapters 20 and 21 together, and I came away with a different thought as to why God will someday be wiping away every tear from our eyes.

The Bible was not originally written with chapters and verse numbers. These were added later by people at least several hundred years after the original text was written for their convenience in referencing a specific passage. With that in mind, if you read Revelations 20:11 to 21:8 at one time without any pause, you may come up with the thought that I did in that the tears that were in our eyes were from what we witnessed at the great white throne judgment. Maybe those tears were for people we saw whose names were not written in the book of life and were cast into the lake of fire (Revelations 20:15). However, maybe those tears were for God our Father who "SO loved"[2] people that He sent Jesus to die for them, yet because of their unbelief, He had to execute judgment on them by sending them to the lake of fire? In other words, we witnessed the God we love doing something He did not want to do to someone He loved SO much. We saw God's pain as He had to send those He loved so much away from Him forever. It's possible that's what produced the tears in our eyes that God wipes away. We saw God's pain and felt for Him.

Is it possible that in our self-centered way of thinking we interpret the Bible as being about us? Thinking only about how everything will impact us? And we don't understand that through the Bible God is trying to share about Himself? Is it possible that God may mourn the death of people much more than we do because of the loss He will feel not having them with Him throughout eternity? Is it possible that while He will wipe away all tears from our eyes and make all things new for us, He will have a spot in His heart that misses those that He has had to send to the lake of fire for eternity? These are questions that will probably not be answered until we see the Lord in heaven, but I believe the answer will be a painful "yes."

While it's a hard memory, I thank the Lord for giving me a glimpse into His heart through the pain I experienced in having to put down a dog that I had loved since it was a puppy. Now that I've had this glimpse into God's heart, I want people to accept Christ, both for their sake as well as for His sake, so that He doesn't have to feel the pain of sending them away from Himself forever.

CHAPTER 19
A CRICKET IN YOUR HAIR?

When my kids were much younger in age, I used to kiss each one of them goodnight once they were in bed. Even if it was brief, it was a good time just to connect with them to let them know I loved them. Most of the times telling them goodnight are blended together in my memory. However, there is one night that is still very memorable to me and probably etched in my mind forever.

My two daughters shared a room together in their early years. As I was kissing one of them, that daughter suddenly screamed in terror. Panic was in her heart (and in mine) until I learned what was causing her panic. My daughter screamed because a cricket had somehow found a way into the house and had jumped on her pillow right next to her head. It was fall, and insects were trying to come in the house to avoid the cold outside.

I quickly caught the cricket, disposed of it and got things back to normal after about five or 10 minutes. During that time, though, there was a lot of stress and anxiety in our house due to a single harmless cricket being inside instead of outside the house. And not just inside the house, but on her pillow and in her hair. As I left their bedroom, I didn't hear an audible voice, but felt the Lord say to me something like, "That [how your daughter reacted to the cricket] is how I want you to react to temptation."

Ponder that one with me for a moment. Now my daughter's reaction was not abnormal for any red-blooded American female. I've seen grown women who have handled childbirth and other very serious matters react in a similar way to a cricket as my daughter did. I think most men would have also had the same reaction as well until they figured out what was on the pillow beside them and they had it out of their hair. Because you weren't there to see my daughter's reaction to the cricket beside her head, picture yourself or someone else you know having this happen to them. This is the mental picture I want you to have as I repeat what I felt the Lord told me: "That is how I want you to react to temptation."

Does that seem a little extreme to you? It did to me too, at first. But after pondering my battle with various temptations since then, if we want to overcome times of temptation, we need to have this very attitude toward temptation when we are tempted.

I am a constant dieter. This means that at times I am successful in watching what I eat and at other times, I don't do very well. You may not be able to tell that about me if we should ever have the opportunity to share a meal together, but inside my head, I am always battling with myself whether it's OK to eat something or not. I have had times of being overweight since my childhood. To have times of success, I must become pretty good at watching what I eat and denying treats and other things offered to me.

At these successful times, I've noticed I am even somewhat militant about it, even possibly hurting the feelings of people who have kindly offered me food by turning them down, not gently, but firmly. I can't please them and lose weight. I have to choose one or the other. If I don't look at that food as I would a cricket on my pillow, I will end up eating the food.

We have biblical examples to support this attitude toward sin.

1. In Genesis 39, the Bible tells us about Joseph who had been sold into slavery to an Egyptian official named Potiphar. Joseph was physically attractive, and Potiphar's wife had taken notice of Joseph. She wanted to sleep with Joseph, and Joseph was doing everything he could to keep from giving in to her. She spoke to Joseph day after day, trying to seduce him. He correctly viewed giving in to her as not only violating his master's trust, but also sinning against God. One day when no one else was around, she cornered him and tried to get Joseph to go along with her advances. What did Joseph do? He ran from her! Just like he would have if a cricket had landed on his pillow.

2. In 2 Samuel 11, David was on his roof and noticed a woman taking a bath. Instead of acting like a cricket had just jumped on his pillow, he stayed there and watched, which eventually led him into adultery and a murderous cover-up of his sin.

3. In Genesis 19, after being instructed by the angels who rescued them to flee and not look back, Lot's wife turns to look back anyway and turns into a pillar of salt. If only she had thought a cricket would get in her hair if she disobeyed the angel and looked back.

In Matthew 5:29–30, Jesus tells His disciples (including us) the following:

> "If your right eye causes you to sin, tear it out and throw it away. For it is better that you lose one of your members than that your whole body be thrown into hell. And if your right hand causes you to sin, cut it off and throw it away. For it is better that you lose one of your members than that your whole body go into hell."

I do not believe Jesus was literally telling us to extract parts of our physical bodies. If He was literally directing us to do this, then there would likely have been mention of the disciples doing it recorded in at least one of the four gospels (Matthew, Mark, Luke and John) or of the early church doing this in the book of Acts. There is not any record of that. However, I do believe He was telling us to take drastic steps to keep ourselves from yielding to temptation, with the earnestness with which we would act if we have a cricket in our hair.

Paul also touched on this when he had heard how the Corinthians responded to his challenge to deal with adultery taking place in their congregation:

> I am no longer sorry that I sent that letter to you, though I was very sorry for a time, realizing how painful it would be to you. But it hurt you only for a little while. Now I am glad I sent it, not because it hurt you but because the pain turned you to God. It was a good kind of sorrow you felt, the kind of sorrow God wants his people to have, so that I need not come to you with harshness. For God sometimes uses sorrow in our lives to help us turn away from sin and seek eternal life. We should never regret his sending it. But the sorrow of the man who is not a Christian is not the sorrow of true repentance and does not prevent eternal death. Just see how much good this grief from the Lord did for you! You no longer shrugged your shoulders but became earnest and sincere and very anxious to get rid of the sin that I wrote you about. You became frightened about what had happened and longed for me to come and help. You went right to work on the problem and cleared it up, punishing the man who sinned. You have done everything you could to make it right.[1]

Paul, in a sense, was complimenting them for acting with the intensity, alarm, and fright as if they had found themselves with a cricket in their hair.

I have encountered many a cricket on my pillow (temptation). Sometimes I've let them stay on my pillow for a while, and then lived to regret it when they jumped in my hair. There was one particular cricket disguised as a unique military computer game which came out years ago that I loved to play. It involved a lot of challenge and strategy, which I enjoy. It soon became a real-life addiction for me as I would find myself still up at 3 a.m. on a workday night still playing it. It was taking precious hours from my life and family.

After several consecutive nights of this and seeing all the things not getting done around the house and me not spending time with my family as I should, I realized I was letting this simple video game overcome me. I cried out to the Lord for forgiveness and help to repent of this. I realized that I had to take drastic measures to end this addiction. Therefore, I gave the disk to my wife, explained to her what had happened and asked her to hide that disk from me. I couldn't just destroy the disk because it belonged to my kids. Thank God, I have not played that game since and not lost countless hours of my life that should be spent with my Lord, family and friends.

The thought of a video game addiction may seem silly to you, but that may be because you don't view video games as a cricket on your pillow. That's OK. But what other things in your life might be a scary cricket that you need to frantically deal with? How about porn on your computer? How about flirting with adulterous relationships? How about all the time you spend on your computer or phone rather than with your family or seeking God? How about greed and valuing money more than you should? Paul urged us, "Don't be greedy, for a greedy person is an idolater, worshiping the things of this world."[2]

Whatever your crickets may be, cry out to God for His help in getting them off your pillow. If you don't, they can get tangled in your hair, work their way into your ear, and then your nose, or worse! Don't begin to think crickets are cute and would make good pets on your pillow and will keep their distance from you. I am being extreme in using this analogy, but as it concerns sin, I am being very serious.

In James 4:7, we are told, "Submit yourselves therefore to God. Resist the devil [Satan], and he will flee from you." Don't resist just a little but resist like there is a cricket trying to invade your right ear! Run like Joseph! Scream like my daughter! Fight like a soldier!

"After all, you have never yet [resisted] struggled against sin and temptation until you sweat great drops of blood."[3] This is speaking of Jesus, when He saw He was moments away from having His beard plucked out, spit upon, struck with fists, having His skin and muscles ripped apart through scourging, and then nailed to a cross.

He sweated great drops of blood due to the temptation He resisted at that time. You see, He could have snapped His fingers and not been crucified. He could have called more than 72,000 angels[4] to come rescue Him so that He wouldn't suffer like He did. However, that wouldn't fulfill God the Father's plan to rescue you and me by Jesus dying in our place. Realize that you will not be the first person to resist temptation with all your might. Jesus had to do it also and understands the intense struggle you may have inside of you in resisting sin.

Ask other Christians to help you with this if needed. It may be humbling to get help, but it may be what it takes for you to get the victory in your battle. I speak from experience. We are told "Confess your sins to each other and pray for each other so that you may be healed. The earnest prayer of a righteous person has great power and produces wonderful results."[5]

I am grateful to the Lord for helping me see how I may have been flirting with various temptations all my life rather than resisting them. In resisting temptations, I've experienced His help in my life. I now know Him better as a result. This is one way we can "know" God.

CHAPTER 20
GOD'S REFRIGERATOR ART

The phrase "refrigerator art" was foreign to me until I became a parent. We had some of our kids' artwork on our refrigerator and someone visiting us referred to it as "refrigerator art." I had to ask them what that term meant. It is artwork a child has drawn or colored that a parent puts on their refrigerator. The artwork is not usually any good, sometimes even just scribbles, but because their child is the one who prepared it, it is proudly displayed on the family's refrigerator.

The central part of Kansas has beautiful sunrises and sunsets. This is because of how flat the terrain is with no nearby mountains, which allows you to see the sun get much lower on the horizon compared to if you live where there are mountains or buildings blocking the horizon. The colors of the sun's rays, especially with some high clouds in the sky, can be so rich.

To some of us that live in Kansas, we view the entire sky at dawn or dusk as God's canvas on which He paints a unique painting for all to enjoy. Human artists can't draw anything as large that seems to surround you when you look at it as God can. If you want to keep the painting, you must take a picture of it because, like clockwork,

God regularly clears the canvas, starts over and paints it all over again the next day.

I didn't always appreciate the sunrise and sunsets in Kansas. I grew up here and they have always been that way. Plus, I'm not an artist and hadn't ever been taught to appreciate colors so much until recently. Someone I know well is very artistic. She explained the unique beauty of a Kansas sunrise and sunset. Since then I have paid attention to them and my friend was right. They are beautiful!

One day I was driving home from work and noticed a sunset that was exceptionally beautiful. I started praising God for it, but then noticed three jet contrails in the sky. It was like these jet contrails were deliberately going through God's artwork and ruined in my mind the perfectness of what God had made. I started talking to the Lord about this explaining why He should be upset with us humans for messing up His beautiful creation. I remember sensing Him quickly tell me in response, "That's my refrigerator art! It's OK."

He then hit me with the realization of how much He loves us. Like any parent loves the art of their children, not because it is beautiful, but because of who drew it. In the same way, God values us more than the beautiful art He draws. He would rather have us using and enjoying His creation rather than us not being around. I am not saying God wants us to pollute the earth. However, He does want us to fill it and subdue it.

While our kids were growing up, our house was littered with toys and things wouldn't always get put away as they should. My wife and I worked hard to keep it clean and in good shape, but there were times when we would look at each other and remind ourselves, "Where no oxen are!" This little phrase would remind us of a big truth. The entire verse goes, "Where no oxen are, the crib is clean. But much increase is by the strength of the ox."[1] This verse is basically saying that things are going to get dirty and messed up if you have oxen in your barn, but it would be better to have that than no oxen in your barn because oxen can produce many good things. We applied this verse to our children and our house. For us, it is much better to have a house lived in by children than to have a house be immaculate.

I believe God has the same feeling toward all of us as my wife and I had toward our children when they were growing up. After hearing Him when I was complaining about the jet contrails in the sky, I now believe that in His eyes it is better to have jet contrails in the sky, footprints in the forest and other signs of human life than to have creation with no sign of human life. We may want to see creation that way, but not Him. He loves our refrigerator art, because He loves us!

CHAPTER 21
COME TO ME!!

As I mentioned earlier, we got our first dog when all of our kids were just about old enough to go to school. When we had to put that dog down a few years later, we went a few months in mourning before getting another dog. This time we got a female golden retriever that we also got as a puppy. What a great dog for our family! About eight years later, my son was given a female black lab that was needing a new home. This black lab had a great pedigree and had been trained well. These two dogs were roughly the same age and they got along with each other well. They even got along great with our two cats! These dogs were valued members of our family. Unfortunately, dogs are like people in that they don't live forever. Both passed away when they were about 13 years old after sharing many great memories with our family. They are forever in our hearts and memories.

About a year went by with no dogs in our lives. Then a family member that had only days earlier acquired a 10-week-old black lab puppy unexpectedly needed someone to keep it for them for about a week. I was available for that week, so with our recent history of well-behaved and well-trained dogs, I agreed to be the main babysitter of this black lab puppy as my wife was needed at her work. I was hoping to relive some of my good memories I had from having the other two dogs.

To protect this puppy's reputation, let's change its name. Let's call her "Flash." That name seems appropriate given the speed at which she could get into mischief.

Soon after Flash arrived, I quickly realized that either I had become a lot older and didn't have the energy and stamina I had years earlier with the other dogs or I had forgotten what having a new puppy with loads of energy was like. I was worn out! Fortunately, we had just put up a new fence around our house and backyard a few months before Flash came to visit. Whereas this wasn't needed with our older dogs, with Flash who didn't know me apart from any other pedestrian, this fence was a life saver.

The first day Flash stayed pretty much within my reach whenever we went into the backyard. When she started to get into something she shouldn't or I needed to get her attention, it was reasonably easy to reach down and touch her. She was starting to respond to her name when I called her, so things were going well. Having a fenced backyard for her was great because it allowed her to be off her leash so she could run, chase balls, and get all that puppy energy out of her system.

One day later in the week, I again had Flash out in our backyard without a leash. She was out of my reach several yards from me. She had found something that I needed to take out of her mouth for her safety. I needed her to come to me. I called her name to get her to come to me, but it didn't work. I tried coaxing her by talking to her softly. I tried acting like I had something in my hands for her. Nothing worked. She was only a few yards from me but avoided my every attempt to get within arm's length of her. I could help her and pet her if she would just get within my reach. I got frustrated. Rather than using the simple command "Come," which had been working until now, out of frustration I found myself slapping my thighs once for each word as I said, "come to me." Looking back on it, I must have thought the slap would punctuate each word so that she would understand it. Or it would emphasize to her how serious I was. I did this a couple times. Just then, as I was saying, "come to me" the third time, it was as if I felt the Lord say those words back to me, with me being the intended listener. He was saying, "Come to me."

At that moment, thoughts flooded my mind of how often I had refused to come to the Lord when He was probably calling "come to me" so He could give me a word of encouragement or otherwise help me, but I didn't hear Him, or rather I chose not to hear Him. Just like Flash was acting like she couldn't hear me. I was too busy, or in my opinion had things under control and didn't need help, or just didn't want to take a time out from my state of busyness to come to Him. Or worse, I didn't want to give up what I was doing or thinking to come to Him. I knew that if I went to Him, He would want me to stop. That was probably what Flash was thinking when I called to her to come to me. Yet, for her best interest, she needed to stop and come to me. In the same way, when the Lord calls me, I need to stop and go to Him.

Two days after that, another thought hit me: Flash must think I have a lot of rules!

- Do this (such as "come" to come to me, "go get it" to chase after the ball, "heel" when I want her to walk with me)
- Don't do that ("hush" when barking at something, "no" when chewing on a dish towel, "no" when chewing on a wooden chair leg or "no" when chewing on a lamp electrical cord)

Yet, I want what's best for her without letting her ruin life for herself or the rest of us.

In the same way, the Lord tells me:

- Do this ("get up" when it's time to get going in the morning and not sleep in, "help them" when I see someone in

need, and "tell them" when I meet someone who may not yet know Jesus and how much He loves them)
- Don't do that ("no" when I want to lose my temper and yell at someone, "no" when wanting to eat more than I should, or "no" when wanting something or someone that I am not to have)

God wants what is best for me and doesn't want to allow me to ruin my life or someone else's.

> God was nailing me with object lessons to help me understand what it feels like to be on His end of our relationship.

Through Flash, God was nailing me with object lessons to help me understand what it feels like to be on His end of our relationship. To see myself through His eyes and what it must be like to be my God. It was a tremendous gift to me to gain that perspective, and I'm very grateful for that. By sharing this with you, I hope you can also see yourself from God's perspective.

I also realize this story may not accomplish for you what it did for me. In your life, this analogy breaks down if those who were supposed to love you instead abused you and took advantage of you. Some of you may feel that some people's dogs are treated better than how you were treated by a parent, another family member or a spouse. My heart goes out to you if that is the case. That is not how it is supposed to be. You may be tempted to blame God for the way you've been treated. I urge you not to blame Him. It's not His fault. That's not how He created relationships to work, but people have messed up what He created so things are not how they are supposed to be. God wouldn't look at all of what creation has become and say, "It is good."

Some of you may ask the question, "If God is so wonderfully powerful, then why couldn't He keep things from being so bad in my life?" That is a great question as so many of us do ask it at some point in our lives. It's difficult to fully answer, but I will offer something to consider.

COME TO ME!!

Looking back at my week with Flash, I could have eliminated any chance that anything would go wrong between her and me by locking her up in her crate all the time. In other words, I could have removed the ability for her to make her own choices. How good for her or me would that be, though? What would her owner who entrusted her to me have thought about me doing that?

As an alternative, I could have kept her on a leash at all times when she was in the backyard so she could never get out of my reach and control. It would have been great for me. If I needed her to get closer to me, all I would need to do would be yank on her leash, forcibly pulling her to me. But that would be miserable for her. She wouldn't be able to explore the fenced backyard with all the grass, trees and flowers. She would miss all the smells that dogs love to smell. She would not get to run at full speed like she was created to do, chasing a leaf blowing in the wind or a ball thrown for her to chase. Essentially, she would have no free will of her own. Furthermore, she would never learn to be without a leash and enjoy all that liberty and then learn to come to me when I call her like my old dogs had done.

My old dogs knew when I called them that they would get a pet on the head or loving words spoken to them or something good to eat. They didn't need a leash to keep them close to me. They might wander away from me, but they didn't ever get too far away. They learned to keep one eye on where I was going and stay within a few seconds' sprint of where I was while they were enjoying their freedom. I enjoyed not having to hold them down with a leash. I enjoyed knowing that I could call them to myself if I felt they were in danger of a nearby car or a threat to a pedestrian walking toward us, if it was time to go home or if I just wanted to show them my love for them by petting and praising them.

You may have heard of the concept of "free will." A way to illustrate "free will" is how I trusted my old dogs to be off a leash even when we were outside our backyard. They would come to me when I called them even though they had a free will not to come to me either. It usually worked out well for both of us because they obeyed my call. Free will didn't work out so well for me or for Flash at this early stage in Flash's life because Flash had not yet learned to obey me. She didn't know that I ultimately wanted what was best for her. Fortunately, I had a fence to keep her within range.

Now imagine billions of Flashes on this planet. Some of them have learned to obey their master. Others have not. Regardless of how much their master calls them, they refuse to come to Him and instead do their own thing. Their own thing is often fighting with other dogs, eating food meant for other dogs, digging in trash cans or chasing skunks. They don't look out after their own pups. In that world, unless you are the biggest dog, life can be miserable.

While it somewhat bothers me to compare humankind to billions of dogs, the comparisons are valid! People can be dogs in the way they treat each other. But if God eliminates our ability to do wrong, He also eliminates our ability to do right out of our free will. Instead, we do what's right because we are forced to do so. If God must force us to do right, isn't this similar to Him keeping us all in crates or on leashes. It won't be what God intended for either Him or us.

I recently listened to a podcast from Pastor Mark Hoover of NewSpring Church in Wichita, Kansas, who said something I had never heard before. He said there was only one thing that you can give God that God doesn't already have. After following Jesus for nearly 50 years, I thought there was nothing I could give God that He didn't already have. God made everything! Couldn't God give Himself whatever He wanted? The Bible clearly says that. What could Pastor Mark be thinking to make such a statement? However, he ended up being right and I was wrong. There is something we can give God that He doesn't already have:

Our trust.

As I've thought more about that podcast, I see the beauty of God's design in creating us with a free will, even if it means we get hurt and we hurt each other. If our world was such so that God forced everyone to do things His way, no one would get hurt. We would be like robots, doing whatever God had programmed us to do. We would trust God always, but only because we could never not trust Him. To not trust Him would violate our programming. So, would we really trust God, or would that be our programming doing its thing? I've concluded that trust without a free will is not trust. It's programming.

But that is not how God made us. How did God make us? Remember, we read it in the first chapter of the first book of the Bible:

God made us "in his own image."[1]

I believe God has a free will, so we have one too. He could have *chosen* not to send Jesus to die on this earth in our place, and just sent us all to hell. No, instead He *chose* to save us from hell and death. Now, the *choice* is ours. We can *choose* to give our *trust* to God, something that He cannot give Himself, or we can *choose* to keep it to ourselves, the *choice* is yours.

There is a third choice some people make. They call it "wait and see." I saw it in Flash's eyes that day when she refused to come to me. She was probably evaluating her options and wanted more time to think about them.

While Jesus encouraged people to "count the cost"[2] before choosing to follow Him, there is a risk that you run out of time to make the decision. God could be like me with Flash and take your pondering His call to you as choosing to reject Him. While God will allow you to make the choice, He doesn't give you eternity to make the decision. Time is shorter than most people think. I urge you that if you do want to take time to "count the cost" like Jesus said, force yourself to make either a "yes" or a "no" decision to trusting Jesus as quickly as possible. Don't let yourself put it off. Besides risking eternal hell if you run out of time, you'll be delaying the start of your eternal life of knowing God. After all, that is what Jesus said eternal life was all about: "Now this is eternal life: *that they know you*, the only true God, and Jesus Christ, whom you have sent."[3]

God is calling to you.

"Come to me!!"

Respond to Him. Trust Him. Know Him. Love Him.

PART THREE
PUTTING IT ALL TOGETHER

CHAPTER 22
ONE GOD

In this book, I have used several names to refer to God: "God," "God the Father," "the Father," "Jesus," "the Son," "the Son of God," "the Creator," and the "Holy Spirit." These terms and how they are used to refer to God can be confusing, making it harder to truly know God. God wants us to love Him with all our heart, with all our soul, and with all our mind.[1] I don't believe God wants us to leave our mind behind in loving Him. So, I want to take a minute to try to eliminate any confusion as to the personhood of God who you are being asked to follow and love.

You might think that by using all these names for God that I, and Christians like me, actually believe in more than one god. That simply is not the case. Wayne Grudem, in his book, "Making Sense of Who God Is" summarizes well what Christians believe about God:

1. God is three persons [Father, Son and Holy Spirit].
2. Each person is fully God.
3. There is one God.[2]

The word "Trinity" is often used to refer to how Christians believe about God. Grudem gives a brief but excellent explanation of the doctrine of the Trinity: "The word *trinity* is never found in the Bible, though the idea represented by the word is taught in many places. The word *trinity* means 'tri-unity' or 'three-in-oneness.' It is used to summarize the teaching of Scripture that God is three persons yet one God."[3]

As simply as I can put it, God is complex. All that He is may be difficult for our limited minds to comprehend. He created us. We did not create Him. If we can't understand fully all of creation (including ourselves), the universe and all that God has made that we can see, how can we expect to fully comprehend God whom we can't see and who made everything we see and touch? He is far above us in every way that we can imagine. Our simple minds, although greatly complex to us, can't be expected to comprehend the Creator who made not only us, but also all of creation that is just as complex to us as we are.

You may be wondering how I can say in this book that "God does _____" or "God loves _____." My only basis for doing so is based on what God has taken the effort to reveal to us about Himself. If He has shared it, we should eagerly believe it. It is our blessing as well as our responsibility to learn all we can about God from what He has revealed about Himself.

Fortunately, we are not required to know everything about God and be able to fully comprehend it in order to know God. There were two men who were crucified at the same time as Jesus, one on each side. One of them scoffed at Jesus. The other one defended Jesus by saying that they deserved to die for their crimes, but that Jesus had done nothing wrong. After that, the one who defended Him simply asked Jesus, "Jesus, remember me when you come into your Kingdom."[4]

This man, who believed Jesus while dying on a cross next to him, probably didn't understand spiritual matters other than that he was a sinner deserving to die, that Jesus did not deserve to die, and that Jesus was our King with a kingdom. Yet, Jesus replied to him, "I assure you, today you will be with me in paradise."[5] We are not required to know all about Jesus to believe in and follow Him. However, we do have to agree with Jesus about who He said He was.

Let's put ourselves in the shoes of Jesus's disciples to see how they may have come to believe that God is three persons (Father, Son and Holy Spirit), that each of these persons is fully God, and there is only one God. Remember that all His disciples were Jews who believed in only one God. How did they come to their belief in God being three persons?

If you were with Jesus and His disciples, you would have witnessed Him doing thousands of miracles. He raised the dead to life several times, one time after the person had been dead and buried for more than three days! He commanded the wind and rain to cease and they immediately obeyed Him. He commanded demons to leave people, and they immediately did what He said. There would have been no doubt in your mind that Jesus was the promised Messiah, meaning the "Anointed One."[6] Your belief would have been confirmed by the prophecies that said when the Messiah was coming,[7] that He would be born of a virgin,[8] and that He would be a descendant of King David.[9] In addition, the powerful prophet John the Baptist said of Jesus, "And I have seen and have borne witness that this is the Son of God."[10]

While you witnessed all these things and believed Jesus was the Messiah,[11] you would have also listened to all the various things He said about Himself:

- "Very truly I tell you," Jesus answered, "before Abraham was born, I am!" (John 8:58, NIV) (Jesus used the same name "I AM" to describe Himself as God did with Moses at the burning bush in Exodus 3:14. This would have been blasphemy for Jesus to say something like this unless He really was God. That is why right after He said this, the crowd picked up stones to stone Him, but Jesus got away from them.)[12]

- "I and the Father are one." The Jews picked up stones again to stone him. Jesus answered them, "I have shown you many good works from the Father; for which of them are you going to stone me?" The Jews answered him, "It is not for a good work that we are going to stone you but for blasphemy, because you, being a man, make yourself God." (John 10:30–33)
- But Jesus remained silent. And the high priest said to him, "I adjure you by the living God, tell us if you are the Christ, the Son of God." Jesus said to him, "You have said so. But I tell you, from now on you will see the Son of Man seated at the right hand of Power and coming on the clouds of heaven." Then the high priest tore his robes and said, "He has uttered blasphemy. What further witnesses do we need? You have now heard his blasphemy." (Matthew 26:63–65)

As one of Jesus's disciples, you would have also witnessed Jesus being worshipped on several occasions by lepers, parents of people Jesus raised from the dead and many others.[13] Even you and the other disciples worshipped Him after He had walked on water, then calmed the storm and got in the boat with you.[14] All of you also worshipped Him when He appeared to you after He was resurrected from the dead[15] and as He ascended into heaven.[16] Jesus accepted the worship rather than deny it. Godly angels and men have always refused to be worshipped.[17]

With Jesus making these statements about Himself, your mind as a Jewish person would have wondered how His statements were consistent with the Shema, the Jewish confession of faith that you had been taught all your life, and which starts out with, "Hear, O Israel: The LORD our God, the LORD is one."[18] You would have also remembered statements made by the God of the Old Testament through the prophet Isaiah, "I am the Lord, that is My name; And My glory I will not give to another,"[19] and also, "Thus says the Lord, the King of Israel, And his Redeemer, the Lord of hosts: 'I am the First and I am the Last; Besides Me there is no God.'"[20] There was room for only one God and one Lord to fit in your beliefs.

If you did not believe what Jesus said about Himself that He was God, you could only conclude that He was crazy (because He wasn't aware that He was saying He was God) or a liar and blasphemer (because He knew He was saying He was God when He actually wasn't God). He couldn't be just a good person, a prophet, or even an angel, because anyone who was good didn't equate themselves with God like Jesus was doing. But how could a crazy lunatic or a blaspheming liar do the miracles He was doing and fulfill prophecy as He did?[21]

If His followers were to believe all that He said and did, they were forced to also believe what Jesus said about Himself was true. Not only was He the promised "Anointed One," "the Son of God," but He was also "Lord," (the Greek word translated from the name of Israel's God "Yahweh" in the Septuagint, the pre-Christian Greek translation of the Old Testament).[22] To call Him "Lord" was the same as calling Him God.

That the disciples believed Jesus was Lord is evidenced by the following:

- After His resurrection, Jesus appeared to a doubting Thomas. "Then he [Jesus] said to Thomas, 'Put your finger here, and see my hands; and put out your hand, and place it in my side. Do not disbelieve, but believe.' Thomas answered him, 'My Lord and my God!'" (John 20:27–28)
- Peter tells a crowd after the Holy Spirit had come, "Let all the house of Israel therefore know for certain that God has made him both Lord and Christ, this Jesus whom you crucified." (Acts 2:36)
- Paul started his letters to the churches with statements similar to the one he used to open the letter to the Romans,

"To all those in Rome who are loved by God and called to be saints: Grace to you and peace from God our Father and the Lord Jesus Christ." (Romans 1:7)

- Paul used statements people made about Jesus to determine if they were speaking in the Holy Spirit or not: "Therefore I want you to understand that no one speaking in the Spirit of God ever says 'Jesus is accursed!' and no one can say 'Jesus is Lord' except in the Holy Spirit." (1 Corinthians 12:3)

- The Apostle John recorded when Jesus appeared to him when he was in exile on the island of Patmos, "When I saw him, I fell at his feet as though dead. Then he placed his right hand on me and said: 'Do not be afraid. I am the First and the Last [God's name from Isaiah 44:6]. I am the Living One; I was dead, and now look, I am alive for ever and ever! And I hold the keys of death and Hades.'" (Revelation 1:17–18, NIV)

Putting ourselves back in the shoes of Jesus's disciples, you as one of His followers will have also remembered hearing other statements Jesus made that indicated He was not the same person as the Father.

- "But concerning that day and hour no one knows, not even the angels of heaven, nor the Son, but the Father only." (Matthew 24:36) [The Father knows something the Son does not.]

- "Do not let your hearts be troubled. You believe in God; believe also in me." (John 14:1, NIV) [Jesus was implying that it was possible to believe in the Father without believing in the Son. Not a good thing to do, but it was possible.]

- "I am the true vine, and my Father is the vinedresser." (John 15:1) [Two different persons]

- "And going a little farther, he [Jesus] fell on the ground and prayed that, if it were possible, the hour might pass from him. And he said, "Abba, Father, all things are possible for you. Remove this cup from me. Yet not what I will, but what you will." (Mark 14:35–36) [He was not praying to Himself when He spent hours in prayer.]

Not only would you have heard that Jesus claimed that He was God, that He was the Son and that He was a separate person from God the Father, you would have also heard Him make statements about the Holy Spirit as God, but as a separate person from the Father and the Son:

- "But the Advocate, the Holy Spirit, whom the Father will send in my name, will teach you all things and will remind you of everything I have said to you." (John 14:26, NIV)
- "And whoever speaks a word against the Son of Man will be forgiven, but whoever speaks against the Holy Spirit will not be forgiven, either in this age or in the age to come." (Matthew 12:32)
- "Go therefore and make disciples of all nations, baptizing them in the name of the Father and of the Son and of the Holy Spirit," (Matthew 28:19)

Looking back at the Old Testament, we can see parts of the Trinity doctrine being revealed, but it was not until Jesus came to earth that it was fully revealed to us. "No one has ever seen God. But the unique One, who is himself God, is near to the Father's heart. He has revealed God to us" (John 1:18, NLT). Jesus stated that no one truly knew the Father except Him, and those to whom He chose to reveal Him.[23] Jesus even told us how we should act to be like our Heavenly Father, giving us more details as to what the heart of God our Father is like.[24]

The disciples of Jesus then taught the same things Jesus taught about the Father, Son and Holy Spirit, relying on the Holy Spirit to help them take Jesus's message to the world after Jesus had returned to heaven. If you read the Book of Acts, you will see the Holy Spirit very involved in this, being referred to many times. He filled people, spoke to people and was lied to by people. In fact, Peter asks someone how they could lie to the Holy Spirit and then says that they didn't lie to people, but to God.[25]

Wayne Grudem explains so well how the New Testament writers expressed their view of the Father, Son and Holy Spirit in the books that follow the four gospels and the Book of Acts:

> When we realize that the New Testament authors generally use the name "God" (Gk. *Theos*) to refer to God the Father and the name "Lord" (Gk. *kyrios*) to refer to God the Son, then it is clear that there is another trinitarian expression in 1 Corinthians 12:4–6: "Now there are varieties of gifts, but the same *Spirit*; and there are varieties of service, but the same *Lord*; and there are varieties of working, but it is the same *God* who inspires them all in every one."
>
> Similarly, the last verse of 2 Corinthians is trinitarian in its expression: "The grace of the *Lord Jesus Christ* and the love of *God* and the fellowship of the *Holy Spirit* be with you all" (2 Cor. 13:14). We see the three persons mentioned separately in Ephesians 4:4–6 as well: "There is one body and one *Spirit,* just as you were called to the one hope that belongs to your call, one *Lord*, one faith, one baptism, one *God and Father* of us all, who is above all and through all and in all."[26]

I realize that this may be a lot to process for our minds. If we would have walked with the disciples and witnessed all the miracles Jesus did, it would have also been a lot for our minds to process.

In all of what God created that we have experienced, 1 +1 +1 = 3. However, God, who was not created, who has no beginning or no end, tells us that He is three persons and that in His being, 1 + 1 + 1 = 1. He doesn't explain to us how that is possible, just that He is what He tells us He is.

With that, I close with something that Jesus said, and ask you if you will believe Him: "Then Jesus told him, 'Because you have seen me, you have believed; blessed are those who have not seen and yet have believed.' Jesus performed many other signs in the presence of his disciples, which are not recorded in this book. But these are written that you may believe that Jesus is the Messiah, the Son of God, and that by believing you may have life in his name."[27]

CHAPTER 23
CONCLUSION

The book of Genesis records the beginning of God's story of His love for humankind. While we read it from our perspective, it is intended to be about Him. It's His story.

God created all of creation, and it was good. This included us. People were special in that they were made in God's own image to rule over creation and to have a loving relationship with God. Instead, they believed a lie and ran from God's presence, bringing a curse on all of creation. Justice required they be sentenced with the same punishment as the devil and his angels who had also previously rebelled against God. The Judge of all the earth must do right.

God has been working ever since to draw humankind back to Himself while also satisfying justice as the Judge of all the earth. It is hard to draw us back to Himself because He made us in His own image, which means that we are not robots with programming but persons with a free will. God will not force anyone to love and obey Him.

People, on the other hand, have been working to satisfy their own desires by doing what is right in their eyes and making a name for themselves, rebelling against God rather than returning to God.

As a result, people hurt and kill each other. This makes God angry to see people hurt by other people, which He views as wickedness. It was this way back in Genesis and is still this way today.

God made a way for us to be rejoined to Him. He determined long ago that the Creator, God the Son (Jesus), would die in man's place in order to satisfy justice, the guiltless one to be given in exchange for the guilty. Only the Creator was guiltless. If a guiltless man could be found, he or she could die in the place of one guilty person, but that wouldn't save anyone else. Only a guiltless Creator could die in the place of all His creation and satisfy justice.

God the Father sent God the Son to this earth to bring to pass this plan of redemption of humankind. God chose a man, Abraham and his descendants through which He would send His Son Jesus, the Creator, and through whom all people of the earth would be blessed. Through Abraham and his descendants, God has revealed His ways, proclaimed prophecies and established patterns that would help us recognize Jesus when He came to fulfill the plan of God.

> **Abraham offering Isaac was the shadow. God offering Jesus was the reality.**

That plan was for Jesus to give up His life for us through His death on a cross. That plan was the reality of what God asked Abraham to do with Isaac until God provided the sacrifice. Abraham offering Isaac was the shadow. God offering Jesus was the reality. Offering Jesus as the sacrifice was the plan of redemption all along. It is the only plan of redemption. There is no other.

God started revealing all of this in Genesis. Genesis is the foundation upon which the rest of God's story of redemption for humankind is written. God reveals more of His story in the history of Israel, as it grows from a new people into a large nation in the Bible books of Exodus through Song of Solomon. Rather than loving God, the nation turns to love others instead. To borrow a phrase from John Eldredge quoting Yancey, reading the books of the prophets Isaiah to Malachi is like "hearing a lover's quarrel through the apartment wall" as God protests Israel's looking for love in others besides Him.

CONCLUSION 181

Matthew through John are four biographies of Jesus's coming to earth where Jesus teaches us about God and offers His life for the sins of the whole world. This is what God has been pointing us to through all the prior books of the Bible. Acts records some of the "acts" of the first followers of Jesus as well as introduces us to the Holy Spirit, the third person of God, who Jesus said His Father would send after Jesus left earth so He would always be with us. The books Romans through 3 John provide further information about God, His plans for us and how we should live in response. Finally, the book Revelation reveals in prophetic code how God intends to finish His redemption of humankind.

Just like us, Jesus wants to be known and loved for who He is, not just what He can do for you. Who wants to be loved just because of their money or power? Just like human love stories, Jesus is like a royal prince looking for His love (you) but doesn't dare show us that He is a prince because people often love princes for their money, prestige and power. So, He humbles Himself and hides His majestic splendor in order to draw those of us who will believe Him, know Him and love Him for who He really is. The end of this age is being held back until all those who will pledge their lives and love to Christ are reached.

If you have yet to decide to follow Jesus, be honest with yourself about why. Recognize and eliminate any biases you may have. Look into the works of former agnostics and atheists who sought to prove Jesus was a fraud but because of the evidence they found now follow Him. Two I recommend are:

- Josh McDowell, *Evidence That Demands A Verdict* at www.josh.org
- Lee Strobel, *The Case for Christ* at www.leestrobel.com

Creation began with one man and one woman choosing not to value the presence of God, hiding from Him when He called out to them. Creation will end with men and women as numerous as the sand on the seashore of every tongue, tribe and nation choosing God's presence in their lives above all else and at all costs. Will you be one of them? Or will you instead be one of those who are punished for unbelief and rebellion with the devil and his angels? You get to decide which one you will be. What will you choose? Please consider Appendix A on the next page.

APPENDIX A
HOW TO BECOME A FOLLOWER OF JESUS

It's really quite simple to become a follower of Jesus Christ. Simply trust Him:

1. <u>Recognize</u> that you have sinned against God and deserve an eternal death.

   a. Romans 3:23, "for all have sinned and fall short of the glory of God."
   b. Romans 6:23, "For the wages [payment for work] of sin is death, but the free gift of God is eternal life in Christ Jesus our Lord."

2. <u>Believe</u> in your heart that Jesus is who He said He is <u>and confess</u> your belief to others. Romans 10:9–10, "If you confess with your mouth that Jesus is Lord and believe in your heart that God raised Him from the dead, you will be saved.

For with the heart one believes and is justified, and with the mouth one confesses and is saved."

That's it! Record the date you do this here to remember it forever! _____

Next, start obeying Jesus's commands as recorded in the Bible:

1. Luke 6:46, "Why do you call me 'Lord, Lord,' and not do what I tell you?"
2. 1 John 5:3, "For this is the love of God, that we keep [obey] his commandments."

Good next steps to obey for any new believer are to do what the first followers of Jesus did: "All the believers devoted themselves to the apostles' teaching, and to fellowship, and to sharing in meals (including the Lord's Supper), and to prayer."[1]

Prayerfully seek a Bible-believing church that can help you with this. They can also explain what baptism is and baptize you in the name of the Father, Son and Holy Spirt, a ceremony involving a public confession of your faith in Jesus. Please contact me at www.lewiserickson.com if you need help finding a church or have questions.

APPENDIX B
DISCUSSION QUESTIONS

Go to www.lewiserickson.com to download these for your small group

ACKNOWLEDGEMENTS

I have learned through this writing experience that writing is a team activity. No longer do I see this as an endeavor of just one person.

As always, I am indebted to my wife, Nancy, for her honest thoughts, encouragement and suggestions. When speaking at a church, ministering to people, writing this book and everything else, you have made me better. Likewise, to my kids, I am grateful for all that God has spoken to me through you. Just a small portion of it is included in this book. Thanks for letting me share it. I am so proud to call you not only my kids, but my brothers and sisters in Christ.

Some friends helped me tremendously by reviewing the first drafts of this book and providing valuable insight and encouragement: Emily, Jenny, Ann, Catherine and Pearl. Emily, your comments to me got this project started. Ann, thank you for investing in me for 24 years and beyond.

Thank you to my editors, Jane VanVooren Rogers and Stacey Wheeler. Is there such a thing as "hazard pay" for editors? Thank you for blessing my readers and me.

I probably wouldn't be at this point in my life if it hadn't been for Pastor Tom Rozof. He opened his pulpit for me to give many messages to the church he founded and trusted me to lead it for a year while he was on sabbatical. He also made Vineyard Leadership Institute available to me so I could be taught by Dr. Steve Robbins and other great theologians. Thank you, Tom.

At the moment when I was struggling the most about whether or not to write this book, I came across a quote from Dr. R. T. Kendall in his book, *40 Days with the Holy Spirit*, that confirmed to me that there needed to be a book written on God the Father. That leads me to the one person who needs to be acknowledged the most: God, the Father, Son, and Holy Spirit. Thank You, Father, for sending Your Son. Thank You, Jesus, for coming. Thank You, Holy Spirit, for always being with us. "To Him Be Glory and Dominion for ever and ever. Amen."[1]

NOTES

Preface

1 Thanks to Pastor Tom Rozof for sharing this quote with our church congregation many times. I was unable to find who first made this quote.

Introduction

1 See Matthew 25:14–30
2 Luke 10:22, NLT, italics added for emphasis.
3 John 17:3, italics added for emphasis.
4 Jeremiah 9:23–24
5 John 14:9
6 See John 17:3
7 See 1 Corinthians 10:6

Chapter 1: The First Turning of the Other Cheek

1 Genesis 1:1
2 Genesis 1:10 and others
3 Genesis 3:1
4 Genesis 3:4–5

5   William Sanford Lasor, *Old Testament survey: the message, form, and background of the Old Testament, 2nd Edition*, (Grand Rapids, Wm. B. Eerdmans Publishing Co., 1982, 1996), 26.
6   Genesis 3:10
7   See Genesis 3:7
8   See Matthew 5:39
9   See Genesis 1:29–30
10 Genesis 3:22– 24
11 See Revelation 12:3–9, Ezekiel 28:13–19, and Isaiah 14:12–15
12 See Revelation 20:10
13 Jude 6
14 Genesis 4:13–14
15 See John 6:37

Chapter 2: Hitting the Reset Button

1   *Abingdon's Strong's Exhaustive Concordance of the Bible*, James Strong, S.T.D, LL.D., Copyright, 1890, by James Strong, Fortieth Printing 1981, ISBN 0-687-40030-9. Hebrew and Chaldee Dictionary word number 7489.
2   Genesis 9:1–7
3   Genesis 6:8

Chapter 4: Blessed, But Do You Know It?

1   Genesis 12:1–3
2   See Genesis 13:13
3   Genesis 15:2, NLT

Chapter 5: Fear Not!

1   See Genesis 15:1
2   See Genesis 21:17
3   See Genesis 26:24
4   See Genesis 46:3
5   See Joshua 11:6
6   See Judges 6:23
7   See 2 Kings 1:15

8   See Daniel 10:12,19
9   See Jeremiah 1:8
10 See Ezekiel 2:6
11 See Luke 1:13
12 See Luke 1:30
13 See Matthew 1:20
14 See Luke 2:10
15 See Matthew 28:5
16 See Acts 18:9
17 See Revelation 1:17
18 Genesis 15:1, NLT
19 Genesis 15:2–3, NLT
20 Genesis 15:4–5, NLT
21 Genesis 15:6, NLT
22 William Sanford Lasor, *Old Testament survey: the message, form, and background of the Old Testament, 2nd Edition*, (Grand Rapids, Wm. B. Eerdmans Publishing Co., 1982, 1996), 49.
23 Ibid.
24 See 2 Timothy 3:12
25 Cole Richards, *The Voice of the Martyrs newsletter*, September 2018, *From the President, "Why We Deny Christ"*, 2.
26 Luke 10:17
27 Luke 10:18
28 Malcolm Smith, *The Blood Covenant: A Study on The Faithfulness of God*, audio tape, (www.malcomsmith.org).
29 See Genesis 15:9–10, NIV.
30 See Genesis 15:17

Chapter 6: God Always Sees Me

1   See Genesis 12:2
2   See Genesis 12:6
3   See Genesis 13:15
4   See Genesis 13:16
5   See Genesis 15:4
6   Genesis 16:2
7   See Genesis 30:1–4.

8   Exodus 3:6
9   Joshua 5:13–15
10 Genesis 16:10–11
11 Psalm 139:11–12, NLT
12 See Genesis 1:3
13 2 Chronicles 16:9, TLB
14 Romans 8:38–39

Chapter 7: One Step at a Time
1   Habakkuk 2:3, TLB
2   Psalm 119:105, KJV
3   All five references are from the ESV, italics added for emphasis.
4   From 1 Kings 19:12, KJV
5   From 1 Kings 19:12, NIV
6   See 1 Kings 19:8–13
7   Mark Batterson, *Whisper: how to hear the voice of God*, (Colorado Springs, Multnomah, 2017), 9–10.
8   Ephesians 6:20

Chapter 8: Your Father is *the* Judge
1   Jane W. Nelson, What Makes a Good Judge?, 9 J. Nat'l Ass'n Admin. L. Judges. (1989) available at http://digitalcommons.pepperdine.edu/naalj/vol9/iss2/5
2   Leviticus 19:15, NLT
3   Revelations 12:9–11, NIV
4   See John 8:44
5   "Abraham Lincoln Had It Right – 'He who represents himself has a fool for a client'", *AVVO*, https://www.avvo.com/legal-guides/ugc/abraham-lincoln-had-it-right---he-who-represents-himself-has-a-fool-for-a-client.
6   See Romans 3:23
7   See Revelation 20:11–15.
8   See 1 John 5:3
9   See Matthew 10:32,33

10. See 1 John 1:9
11. See Luke 6:46
12. Luke 14:26–27
13. See Romans 1:16
14. See Matthew 10:33
15. See Luke 6:46–49
16. See Acts 4:12
17. See Luke 8:14
18. See Hebrews 5:8
19. See John 16:26,27
20. See John 3:16–17
21. See Titus 1:2
22. See Hebrews 1:2, Colossians 1:16, John 1:3
23. See Genesis 1:26
24. See 2 Corinthians 5:21
25. Luke 22:31–32, NIV
26. See Job 1:8–12
27. Romans 15:30, NIV

Chapter 9: Judge, Jury and Executioner

1. See Genesis 9:6
2. See Romans 13:1–4
3. Romans 12:19, TLB
4. Genesis 18:20
5. *Abingdon's Strong's Exhaustive Concordance of the Bible*, James Strong, S.T.D, LL.D., Copyright, 1890, by James Strong, Fortieth Printing 1981, ISBN 0-687-40030-9. Hebrew and Chaldee Dictionary word number 2201, 2199 and 6618.
6. "Archaeologists Claim to have Discovered the Location of the Biblical City of Sodom", *Ancient Origins*, https://www.ancient-origins.net/news-history-archaeology/archaeologists-claim-have-discovered-location-biblical-city-sodom-004148.
7. See Genesis 19:9
8. Genesis 19:17, NIV
9. See Genesis 19:22

10 See 2 Peter 2:7–8
11 2 Peter 3:9, NLT
12 See Luke 9:54–56
13 See Hebrews 1:3, NLT
14 Luke 13:6–9, NLT
15 Luke 5:11

Chapter 10: He Takes It Personally

1 God changed Abram's and Sarai's names to Abraham and Sarah in Genesis chapter 17.
2 Genesis 20:2, NIV
3 Romans 1:20, NIV
4 See Genesis 1:31
5 Psalm 51:4, NIV
6 Acts 9:4–5, NIV

Chapter 11: It Comes to Pass

1 See Genesis 17:19
2 *Abingdon's Strong's Exhaustive Concordance of the Bible*, James Strong, S.T.D, LL.D., Copyright, 1890, by James Strong, Fortieth Printing 1981, ISBN 0-687-40030-9. Hebrew and Chaldee Dictionary word number 3327.
3 Genesis 21:6, NIV
4 See Genesis 21:11
5 Genesis 21:10, NIV
6 Genesis 21:12–13, NIV
7 Genesis 21:14, NIV
8 See Genesis 21:14
9 Matthew 7:7, NIV

Chapter 12: How God Felt

1 Wikipedia contributors, "Empathy," Wikipedia, The Free Encyclopedia, https://en.wikipedia.org/w/index.php?title=Empathy&oldid=909611540 (accessed August 7, 2019)

2 Genesis 22:1–2
3 Genesis 22:10
4 Genesis 22:12
5 Genesis 18:17–18
6 Genesis 22:12
7 1 John 4:19, KJV

Chapter 13: Turning Things Upside Down

1 Genesis 25:23
2 See Genesis 25:22
3 See Genesis 48:12–20
4 See 1 Samuel 16:1–13
5 1 Samuel 16:7, TLB
6 1 Samuel 16:11, NIV
7 1 Samuel 16:12, NIV
8 1 Samuel 16:7
9 See 1 Peter 3:3–4, KJV and NLT
10 See Job 5:11–13
11 See John 17:2–3
12 See John 15:4–6
13 Hebrews 1:3, NIV
14 See Matthew 20:16, Mark 10:31 and Luke 13:30
15 See Matthew 6:33
16 Revelation 3:17, TLB

Chapter 14: Holding on

1 See Genesis 26:2–5
2 See Genesis 28:13–16
3 See Genesis 33:9,15 and 36:6–8
4 See Genesis 28:13–16
5 See Genesis 28:20–22
6 See Genesis 29, 30 and 31:3–21
7 See Genesis 31:1–2
8 See Genesis 20:3–7

9. See Genesis 31:24, 29
10. See Genesis 32:1
11. See Genesis 32:3–21
12. See Genesis 32:22–32
13. See Genesis 33
14. See Genesis 34
15. See Genesis 35:1
16. See Genesis 35:2–29
17. See Proverbs 19:3
18. Genesis 32:30
19. Genesis 32:1
20. See Genesis 28:10–15
21. See Hebrews 7:7
22. See Genesis 25:22
23. See Genesis 25:26
24. Dr. Steve Greene, *Invisible Limp*, (Charisma, March 2019), page 8.
25. See Genesis 29:18–30
26. See Genesis 31:5–13
27. Genesis 32:28 NLT, Italics added for emphasis.
28. Genesis 35:10 NLT
29. See Genesis 18
30. See Revelation 22:8–9
31. See Joshua 5:13–15
32. See Judges 13:2–25
33. See Judges 13:18
34. See Luke 1:19
35. See Exodus 34:5–7
36. See Matthew 6:9
37. See John 3:16, John 16:27 and many, many other verses.
38. See John 15:18–27
39. Nigel Briggs, © 2003 Vineyard Songs (UK/Eire) (Vineyard Music UK)

Chapter 15: Working All Things Together

1. See Genesis 29:31

2 Genesis 30:8, NLT
3 Genesis 30:22, NLT
4 Genesis 37:3
5 Genesis 37:4
6 See Genesis 50:19–21
7 See Genesis 43:32 and Genesis 46:34
8 See Matthew 25:41
9 Proverbs 19:3, NLT
10 Matthew 5:11,12 NLT
11 Romans 8:28

Chapter 16: Judah: From Wickedness to the Heart of Jesus
1 See Luke 15:11–32
2 See Genesis 43:8
3 Genesis 42:38, NIV
4 Genesis 43:9, NIV
5 Genesis 44:33–34, NIV
6 See Genesis 45:1–3
7 See Luke 10:22
8 See Luke 15:11–32

Chapter 18: Much More Than Puppy Love
1 Act 17:28, KJV
2 See John 3:16, KJV

Chapter 19: A Cricket in Your Hair?
1 2 Corinthians 7:8–11, TLB
2 Colossians 3:5, NLT
3 Hebrews 12:4, TLB
4 See Matthew 26:53
5 James 5:16, NLT

Chapter 20: God's Refrigerator Art
1 Proverbs 14:4, KJV

Chapter 21: Come to Me!!

1. Genesis 1:27
2. See Luke 14:25–33
3. John 17:3, NIV

Chapter 22: One God

1. See Matthew 22:37
2. Wayne Grudem, *Making Sense of Who God Is*, (Grand Rapids, Zondervan, 1994), 120.
3. p 115–116.
4. See Luke 23:39–42
5. See Luke 23:43
6. *Abingdon's Strong's Exhaustive Concordance of the Bible*, James Strong, S.T.D, LL.D., Copyright, 1890, by James Strong, Fortieth Printing 1981, ISBN 0-687-40030-9. Hebrew and Chaldee Dictionary word number 4899.
7. See Daniel 9:25–26. See also Josh McDowell, *Evidence That Demands A Verdict Revised Edition*, (San Bernardino, 1979), 170–175 for a detailed computation from the decree of Artaxerxes to Nehemiah on March 5, 444 B.C. to March 30, A.D. 33, Jesus's triumphal entry into Jerusalem fulfilling this prophecy.
8. See Isaiah 7:14
9. See Jeremiah 23:5
10. John 1:34
11. See John 6:68–69
12. See John 8:59
13. Matthew 8:2, 9:18, Mark 5:6, John 9:38
14. Matthew 14:32–33
15. Matthew 28:17
16. Luke 24:52
17. Acts 10:25–26, 14:11–18, Rev 19:10, 22:9
18. Deuteronomy 6:4. See also "Jewishness and the Trinity", *Jews For Jesus*, (https://jewsforjesus.org/articles/?authors=Arnold.Fruchtenbaum&AUID=MTU5MA==), The Shema, p 6.
19. Isaiah 42:8, NKJV

20. Isaiah 44:6, NKJV
21. This "trilemma" that Jesus was either a liar, a lunatic or Lord was presented by C.S. Lewis and later by Josh McDowell, *Evidence That Demands A Verdict Revised Edition*, (San Bernardino, 1979), 103.
22. *The Holy Bible, Today's New International Version*™ TNIV. ® Copyright © 2001, 2005 by International Bible Society ®. All rights reserved worldwide. Page 1914, footnote 10:9.
23. See Luke 10:22
24. See Matthew 5:43–45
25. See Acts 5:3–4
26. Wayne Grudem, *Making Sense of Who God Is*, (Grand Rapids, Zondervan, 1994), 120.
27. John 20:29–31, NIV

Appendix A: How to Become a Follower of Jesus
1. Acts 2:42, NLT

Acknowledgements
1. I Peter 5:21, KJV

Made in the USA
Monee, IL
03 May 2026

49437773R00115